UNIVERSITY OF NORTH CAROLINA
STUDIES IN THE ROMANCE LANGUAGES AND LITERATURES

Number 121

GOLDEN AGE DRAMA IN SPAIN:
GENERAL CONSIDERATION AND
UNUSUAL FEATURES

GOLDEN AGE DRAMA IN SPAIN:
GENERAL CONSIDERATION AND UNUSUAL FEATURES

BY

STURGIS E. LEAVITT

CHAPEL HILL
THE UNIVERSITY OF NORTH CAROLINA PRESS

DEPÓSITO LEGAL: V. 2.589 - 1972
ARTES GRÁFICAS SOLER, S. A. - JÁVEA, 28 - VALENCIA (8) - 1972

TABLE OF CONTENTS

		Pages
LIST OF ABBREVIATIONS		9
FOREWORD		11
I.	The Popular Appeal of Golden Age Drama in Spain	13
II.	Spanish *comedias* as Pot Boilers	24
III.	Lions in Early Spanish Literature and on the Spanish Stage.	40
IV.	Strip-Tease in Golden Age Drama	48
V.	Scenes of Horror in Golden Age Drama	55
VI.	Some Aspects of the Grotesque in the Drama of the Siglo de Oro	59
VII.	Notes on the *gracioso* as a Dramatic Critic	71
VIII.	The *gracioso* takes the Audience into his Confidence	75
IX.	Lope de Vega and the New World	80
X.	A Maligned Character in Lope de Vega's *El mejor alcalde el rey*	87
XI.	Divine Justice in the *Hazañas del Cid*	91
XII.	A Note on the *Burlador de Sevilla*	98
XIII.	Did Calderón have a Sense of Humor?	101
XIV.	Humor in the *autos* of Calderón	104
XV.	Pedro Crespo and the Captain in *El alcalde de Zalamea*	118
XVI.	Cracks in the Structure of Calderón's *El alcalde de Zalamea*.	121
XVII.	Some Fields for Further Research in Golden Age Drama	125

LIST OF ABBREVIATIONS

Acad	*Obras de Lope de Vega,* publicadas por la Real Academia Española, 15 vols. (Madrid, 1890-1913)
AcadN	*Obras de Lope de Vega,* publicadas por la Real Academia Española, nueva ed., 13 vols. (Madrid, 1916-1930)
BAE	Biblioteca de Autores Españoles
BH	Bulletin Hispanique
CHA	Cuadernos Hispanoamericanos
NBAE	Nueva Biblioteca de Autores Españoles
PMLA	Publications of the Modern Language Association of America
Rev.	Revista
RFE	Revista de Filología Española
RPh	Romance Philology

FOREWORD

The articles in this volume dealing with Golden Age drama in Spain have appeared in various journals and homage publications, not all of them easy of access. It has, therefore, seemed worth while to put them all together, with a few minor changes, in the hope that they may be found useful to those who are interested in the flowering of dramatic production in Spain.

Some of the articles deal with unusual, and seemingly unimportant, features of the plays of the period, but they all contribute to an understanding of the complexity of Golden Age drama and an appreciation of what the *comedias* and *autos sacramentales* meant to the audiences of the time.

Some repetition will be apparent in the collection, but this may serve to emphasize the point under discussion.

The original place of publication is indicated at the end of each article.

S. E. L.

Chapter I

THE POPULAR APPEAL OF GOLDEN AGE DRAMA
IN SPAIN

The title of this article precludes any analysis of the literary qualities of one of Spain's most glorious possessions. By the same token, no comparison can be made here between the plays of seventeenth century Spain and those of other countries. Nor can this article include any study of the dramatic technique of the period, free as it was from the restrictions of the famous unities of time, place, and action.

It is possible that an explanation of the popularity of the drama of the Golden Age in Spain may seem to imply unfavorable criticism of the plays themselves. Such an interpretation is definitely not intended. The point of view which has been taken is not that of a dramatic critic, literary connaisseur, or anything of the sort. It merely assumes that a play is something to be presented before an audience that pays admission; that a play should have in it certain elements that will please this audience; and, that in the case at hand it is possible to conjecture what these elements were, basing our conclusions on some knowledge of Spanish character and on some acquaintance with the theater of today.

The dramatic production in Spain during what is commonly called the *Siglo de Oro* exceeds in quantity that of any other nation during the same period. Indeed, the number of plays produced in the Spanish Golden Age is perhaps greater than that of any country during a similar span of years. Spanish plays of that unbelieveably exuberant period could be counted, if anyone cared to engage in such an exercise, not in hundreds, but in thousands. One might, without too much impropriety, use the term "astronomical figures" in referring to the total reckoning.

A few examples will throw light on the above statements. At the age of forty-one the great master of them all, Lope de Vega, stated that he had written 230 plays; six years later the number had grown (so he says) to 483; and sixteen years after this (again on his testimony), to 1070. Is it any wonder that his biographer, Juan Pérez de Montalván, also something of a dramatist in his own right, with over 150 plays to his credit, claimed that Lope de Vega had written 1800 full length plays and 400 autos (one act religious pieces) during his lifetime. To be sure, some critics have questioned the arithmetic of both Lope de Vega and Montalván, and wondered whether it was altogether trustworthy. But we must not be too hasty in disputing these statistics when we remember that there are some five hundred plays of Lope now available in spite of the ravages of time.

Another playwright, Tirso de Molina, boasts of having written more than 400 *comedias,* of which we have only about eighty today. If the Consejo de Castilla had not decided that an ordained priest, such as Tirso was, should not write any more plays (His were a public scandal, so the records state.), the chances are that Tirso would have become a serious rival of Lope's in mass production. With these two men, plays seem to come off an assembly line. Calderón de la Barca wrote some 120 plays and 80 religious pieces. The men mentioned are the outstanding dramatists of the period, but there were innumerable minor playwrights to swell the grand total of plays to figures that simply stagger the imagination.

The enormous production of Lope de Vega can be explained in terms of extraordinary genius. The same can be said with somewhat less certainty, perhaps, of Tirso de Molina and Calderón. But the vast number of plays by all authors, great and small, finds its principal explanation in the support received from people who went to see them. There would have been some sort of a theater in Spain in the seventeenth century, if there had been only a few spectators, but drama would not have reached such vast proportions without the constant encouragement of men and women who paid money for entertainment they liked. There would be football today, if there were no tickets bought by thousands of spectators, but it would be a different kind of football. It would not be the national institution that it is. Neither would the *comedia* in seventeenth century Spain have become a national institution without the active support of the public.

Football coaches of today usually receive a straight salary for their services, and the playwrights of the Golden Age sold their product outright for as good a price as they could get. Nevertheless, football coaches of today are probably not unmindful of gate receipts, and the probability is that dramatists of the seventeenth century in Spain were not altogether oblivious to the box-office. It would be strange indeed if a reputation gained by previous performances did not affect the size of the sum collectable for coaching or for plays. Furthermore, like the football coach of today, the Spanish author doubtless took no small satisfaction in being something of a popular hero. If he ever attained that distinction, he tried to live up to his reputation by keeping up his output.

It will not be amiss to refresh our minds about the conditions under which the plays of the Golden Age were presented to an enthusiastic public. Performances were held in courtyards (*corrales*), or large spaces between buildings. The stage itself was a rough structure erected at one end of the courtyard; a few bleacher-like seats extended down the sides; there was a gallery in the back for women only; the people of consequence viewed the show from windows overlooking the courtyard; and the great body of the audience, made up of people of humble estate, enjoyed the privilege of standing room, unless they wanted to pay extra for a seat on one of a few moveable benches in front. Only the stage and what we may call the bleacher seats were covered with a roof. An awning (*toldo*) protected the "standees" from the sun, but this covering could hardly have been effective in case of rain. There was no front curtain, no stage furniture to speak of, no painted back drops, no special lighting effects. Plays began at four in the summer and at two in the winter. The audience was supposed to be out of the theater before dark, probably to make it easier for the police to suppress noisy demonstrations.

It cannot be said that the spectators went to the theater to find a cool spot in summer or a warm seat in winter, as is the case now with some people who frequent our air-cooled and steam-heated movie palaces. The terribly oppressive heat of Madrid in summer could hardly have been tempered to any great extent by the awning.

In this connection it is interesting to recall that the women's gallery was most appropriately called the *cazuela,* or stew pan. In winter the icy cold of Madrid could hardly have been anything but painfully present in the minds of the shivering spectators as they witnessed the performance scheduled for the day. Before the show, however, they had something to entertain themselves with, if they had money to buy it from concessionaries—nuts, oranges, or cucumbers in season, to be washed down with *aloja,* a sweet drink which may roughly be compared to our omnipresent Seven-Up or Coca-Cola. After the repast, the orange peelings and nut shells served a most useful purpose, if one of the spectators wanted to throw something at the women in the gallery, or if he felt inclined to register active disapproval of the actors at some stage of the performance.

The show might begin with a *loa,* an introductory piece which served to call the audience to order and put it in a proper frame of mind. This *loa* might have something by way of explanation of the plot of the play to come, it might flatter the audience by complimentary remarks, or it might arouse their laughter by a well directed joke or two. It doubtless served to break the ice much better than the modern orchestra, which used to play a couple of tunes before the curtain rose. After the *loa* came the *comedia,* a three act play in verse. Between the acts there was dancing and singing, or a short comic skit called an *entremés.* These *entremeses* roughly corresponded to our cartoons or short comics, and the singing and dancing to the vaudeville acts which sometimes grace our movie palaces. The afternoon's performance might end with a *fin de fiesta,* a light piece which put everyone in good humor before going home.

No doubt these between-the-acts performances had their fair share of the audience's approval, especially the dances. There were some, the *escarramán* and the *zarabanda,* which seem to have been quite sensational. How startling they would be in the hard-boiled world of today is another question. In those times they not infrequently shocked some sensitive souls who promptly exercised their influence to have such scandalous exhibitions suppressed. But the public demand was usually vocal enough to bring the dances back after a suitable period of banishment or surgical treatment.

It must be confessed that a perusal of the between-the-acts pieces, the *entremeses*, does not reveal anything particularly exciting either in action or situation. Except for those written by Cervantes, and which he says were never played, the majority of these one act plays have relatively little interest. But doubtless the actors compensated for the defects with appropriate buffoonery, and made an otherwise insipid piece seem the height of humor. Examples of similar instances in our glorious movie tradition are unnecessary here.

The main show was the real pay-off, and to it we must devote our major attention. At first sight, it is hard for an American audience to conceive that a play in verse—and all the *Siglo de Oro* plays were in verse—could be a major attraction. Certainly, verse plays on the American stage would stand about the same chance as the proverbial snow ball in an oft-mentioned other world. It was definitely not that way in the Golden Age in Spain. Let us see why.

It may be said without fear of sucessful contradiction that the main body of the audience of those times was no more highbrow than the average movie audience of today. On the contrary, the "musketeers," as the "standees" were appropriately called, could not have attained a high IQ rating by any test. They were an uneducated, unruly lot; their feet were tired; they were uncomfortably hot or cold, according to the season; they had paid good money to see the show, one half a *real,* the equivalent of a dozen oranges or a half dozen eggs today, and they expected their money's worth. They were hard to please. Authors and actors alike were afraid of them. They had reason to be.

Whith this audience very much in mind, the playwrights of that day provided the most important element in any play—action. Things *happen* in the Golden Age plays. There are battles between whole armies, and we are permitted to see isolated and realistic fragments, or else witness the entire spectacle through the eyes of an interested character who describes the battle blow by blow. There are tournaments, there are duels and murders. Ghosts rise from the dead to give prophesies, or to warn guilty people that they are doing wrong. Men and women are killed before our eyes with all kinds of weapons, and blood spouts from gaping wounds. Corpses sometimes litter the stage to such an extent that their presence must have made for hard walking. There is no record, though, of broken legs caused by stumbling over dead bodies or slipping in beet juice or cheap claret. Perhaps the annals of the stage failed to record such common occurrences.

With no limitations imposed by stage sets, as is the case today, the playwright of that period was at liberty to present by suggestion an infinite variety of scenes, leaving it to the imagination of the audience to supply the details. An elevated place in the back of the stage might represent a tower, a wall of a city, a high hill, or the second story of a house with its balcony. The audience was supposed to imagine that the actors were in a garden, a wood, on a battle field, or at the seashore. The spectators could never have been disappointed in the scenery, since it existed principally in their imagination. The great advantage to the author lay in the fact that, like the scenario writers of today, he was unrestricted in his choice of locale. He did not have to limit each act to a single setting. For him the world was his stage, as it is in Hollywood now.

A favorite arrangement of conflicting interests is the peasant-overlord-king combination. The overlord oppresses the peasant, who naturally enough is one of nature's noblemen. A heart of gold beats warmly beneath his rugged cloak. The King takes the side of the peasant and sees that justice is done, or else endorses the underdog's interpretation of personal vengeance. It is indeed true that sometimes the peasant turns out to be a nobleman in disguise, but even so, the nobleman's stay in rural areas has been of great benefit to him. It has endowed him with the traditional heart of gold, so characteristic of simple life. In plays like these the "musketeers" see themselves in the role of nature's nobleman, and they take sides in the conflict, as is proper. They applaud in the right places, as they should.

National heroes pass back and forth across the stage, and a thrill of patriotism is aroused, just as when an American flag is raised in our theater today. We see Guzmán el Bueno remain loyal to his trust and throw his own dagger to the Moors when they threaten to kill his son, if he does not surrender the city. (The Moors, let it be said, make use of this weapon.) We see Pedro el Justiciero mingling with his people and dispensing justice in no uncertain manner. We see the rise to power of the great Álvaro de Luna, and his eventual downfall. We see María de Molina thwart the schemes of wicked nobles and put her son on the throne in spite of determined and unscrupulous opposition. We see the Catholic Sovereigns, Ferdinand and Isabella, intervene in many a situation and win the sympathy of the audience by their integrity and courage. And of course there is the national hero, Ruy Díaz de Vivar, taking up his father's cause, even to his own personal loss, and avenging in blood an unforgiveable affront. Later, this same individual wins a pitched battle against four Moorish kings, who in reverence call him "Mío Cid." Still later, and not altogether to our surprise, this same Cid proves that he is not merely a leader of soldiers but a man of personal courage, for he offers to fight a regular giant of a man whom everybody else fears. It is quite gratifying to the audience to see their hero return in triumph from the ensuing trial by single combat. Not content with introducing these feats of arms, the author of this extraordinary play has the Cid show compassion to a leper and eat out of the same plate with him, to the amazement of his men, who are literally sick to the stomach at the horrid sight. The Cid not only gives this demonstration of applied Christianity, but preaches a good sermon on the subject. What more could any audience ask than this?

There are love stories galore where boy meets girl, and hero and heroine scheme mightily to thwart the vigilance of a father or brother. In these *capa y espada,* or cape and sword plays the lovers meet surreptitiously on the street, in a church, or even up in Mabel's room, always on the verge of being discovered by the watchful guardian. Clever ways are devised to send messages, plan rendezvous, or concoct disguises. Before the girl is won, the plot becomes as complicated as diagrams of football tactics. It is easy to suppose that the audience was properly impressed by such a display of ingenuity, just as it would be today.

The usual practice is to introduce, even in the tragic plays, a humorous character who carries on a love affair parallel to that of his master. In the course of this character's career all kinds of humor are introduced —puns, jokes, stories, wisecracks, and generally comic remarks. Sometimes, the *gracioso,* as this character was called, is ignorant; but just the same he is nobody's fool, for at some point in the play he surprises everybody by seeing clearly where all the rest are blind. Sometimes, the *gracioso* is as bright as his master, and has a large share in planning the love campaign.

His principal part in the play, however, is to react to situations with homely common sense and a touch of humor. In the case of Tirso de Molina the *gracioso* is vulgar in the extreme, but such lack of decency is not a common practice with other playwrights. For the most part the *gracioso* is just good clean fun. If by any chance the "musketeers" should fail to appreciate the intricacies of the plot or the noble sentiments expressed by the main characters, they were practically sure to have a good time with the *gracioso*. For the author, this character was a sort of anchor in the wind, an emergency insurance against unfavorable reaction to the play.

The *gracioso* is not the only comic character in the drama of seventeenth century Spain. At times a whole play is built up around an excentric figure provocative to laughter. In one case he may be an inveterate liar who comes to be suspected even when he tells the truth; in another, he may be a man who loves comfort above all things, and makes a philosophy out of it; in another, he may be a fop who is convinced that all the ladies swoon at the mere sight of him; or again, he may be a wealthy old codger just returned from America and ready to fall a prey to some designing male or female. In most cases he is a man from outside the capital, like Lucas del Cigarral, thus described:

> "He is pale; his hands are like those of anybody else; his feet are a little long, but they are flat and wide, with corns and bunions; he is a little bit knock-kneed; two little bits dark green in complexion; three little bits careless in his dress; and forty little bits dirty. If he sings in the morning, as the proverb goes, he not only frightens away his own troubles but those of his neighbors. If he takes a nap in his country estate, he snores so loud they hear him in the city. He eats like a student; drinks like a German; asks as many questions as a nobleman; and talks like a man who has just inherited property...."

In many cases the plays were enlivened by rural scenes where peasants dance and sing. No doubt these scenes were attractive in the extreme, with much movement, with bright costuming and cheerful with catchy music. In this connection we may recall the popular opera *Oklahoma,* and imagine what it would be like to see snatches of it interspersed at suitable moments in a serious play. Nature's noblemen, hearts of gold, and *Oklahoma* would be hard to beat anywhere.

No little stress is put upon what is known as *pundonor.* According to this convention, husbands are painfully jealous of their wives and are quick to avenge in blood what may be only an appearance of guilt. If this high handed punishment came as a result of insane jealousy, we of today would be more sympathetic; but the killing is decidedly a cold blooded affair. To an audience of today, at least to an American audience, this unwritten law is decidedly repellent, but in seventeenth century Spain it had its popular appeal. Such fare is too strong for Americans and we are glad to turn our eyes away, just as we do when the horses are killed in the bull fight. But we must remember that bull fights are Spanish, and so is *pundonor.* It was a Spanish audience that was witnessing the play.

At the end of many of the tragic plays the author frequently introduces a surprise effect that would send cold chills down the spine of any audience. The stage designers of that day had invented a neat little device in the absence of a front curtain. A small curtain in the back of the stage concealed an alcove or back room which could be used to good effect at an opportune moment. The curtain would be pulled aside to disclose a lighted altar richly decorated with all its accessories, or to show a King upon his throne in regal attire and surrounded by the pomp befitting his office. More often, this curtain, when drawn aside, gave the audience a glimpse of a dead man in a particularly gruesome condition—his throat cut from ear to ear, or a garrote about his neck. The use of this back parlor was optional, however, because we have these impressive and horrible sights on the stage itself; as for example, in the second half of the Cid play referred to, when King Sancho is brought in, pierced through with a javelin—and still alive! It is interesting to note that when these same plays are presented today, the scenes of horror are greatly toned down. The garroted man becomes, for example, a shrouded figure dimly visible between two lighted candles. Evidently, the audiences of the Golden Age were fonder of red meat than the Spanish audience of today. The realism of the *Siglo de Oro* is too strong a dish for the twentieth century.

In general, the plays of the seventeenth century in Spain are saturated with national spirit and Spanish tradition. Much emphasis is put upon honor and personal vengeance, loyalty to the King, religious feeling, nobility in thought and in deed, respect for women, praise of simple life, and national customs. All these are good drama and excellent drawing cards anywhere. And if we add to these qualities constantly recurring humor, the recipe is complete.

In his famous play, *The Bashful Man at Court,* Tirso de Molina accurately describes the popular appeal of the plays of his day:

> "In a *comedia* are not the eyes delighted to see a thousand things that make people forget their troubles? Does not music delight the ear? Does not the discreet man enjoy the concepts and the inventions? Isn't there laughter for the happy man? Isn't there sadness for the sad, and wit for the witty? Is not the stupid man enlightened, and the ignorant man taught? Isn't there war for the brave, advice for the prudent, and authority for the wise? If one wants Moors, there are Moors; if one desires tournaments, there are tournaments; if bull fights, bull fights are provided...."

The public of the seventeenth century found in the theater a means of escape from the humdrum of daily life, just as the working girl of our times finds in the movies a dream world in which to move vicariously for a few brief hours. The public of that day wanted new plays, just as the movie audiences of ours are avid for new shows. It did not much matter whether the same situation was served up again in different dress. It does not matter today when stock situations and plots are only thinly disguised. The audience wants action, excitement, an afternoon's diversion at a moderate price. In fact, the situation in the Golden Age in Spain was as much like the movie situation today as is possible to imagine. With the tremendous popular demand for new plays, the authors worked day and night to supply it. They are doing it now in Hollywood.

It would seem that the dramatists of the Golden Age in Spain should have lived in our times, so they could have written for the movies. Had they been thus privileged, they would have indeed made more money than they did in Spain. But they would not have been any happier. The movie magnates of Hollywood would certainly have mutilated their product to such an extent that the authors would have disowned their own children. As it was, they had only the public to please. How much better that they lived when they did, wrote as they did, and that we have the opportunity to read what they actually put on paper.

Fourth Series. *Lectures in the Humanities, 1947-1948. University of North Carolina Extension Bulletin, XXVIII* (January 1949), No. 3, 7-14.

Chapter II

SPANISH *COMEDIAS* AS POT BOILERS

The *comedias* of the Golden Age in Spain present a field of investigation that seems to be inexhaustible. The dramatic productions of that unbelievably exuberant period are so numerous that no one can hope to read them all. Even to try to keep up with the research based upon them is a task of the first magnitude. These plays have been studied from the point of view of sources, dramatic technique, versification, style, dates of the plays, authorship, and much, much else.

But there is one point of view that has hardly been seen by critics, or, in my opinion at least, has not received the attention it deserves. This is consideration of the plays as saleable items, as a source of quick money, as a means of getting cash to buy groceries with, to pay the rent, to keep the wolf from the vestibule.

In this connection, let us first consider Lope de Vega's *Arte nuevo de hacer comedias en este tiempo*, read before a loosely organized and probably aristocratic group called the "Academia de Madrid."[1] This poem consists of what seems at first sight to be an apology for Lope's manner of writing plays, and then an explanation in considerable detail of how he would like them to be, all this cluttered up with an empty display of erudition which perhaps was intended to flatter his hearers, or to stupefy them into a helpless collapse.

---

[1] "Sans doute quelqu'une de ces assemblées littéraires, imitées de celles qui fleurissaient alors en Italie et qui tenaient leurs séances chez quelque grand seigneur lettré." Alfred Morel-Fatio, "L' 'Arte nuevo de hacer comedias en este tiempo' de Lope de Vega," *BH*, III (1901), 367.

Let us see what Lope says about his subject and how he says it. He begins by addressing his audience as "ingenios nobles, flor de España." He continues:

> Fácil parece este sugeto, y fácil
> Fuera para cualquier de vosotros,
> Que ha escrito menos dellas, y más sabe
> Del arte de escribirlas y de todo.

What a ridiculous statement, if taken seriously! What did these "ingenios nobles" know about writing plays? Lope here is being polite—Spanish style.[2] He then continues in another vein, saying that he is not ignorant of the "preceptos," but he has observed in regard to plays that: "Quien con arte las escribe / Muere sin fama y galardón."

As to his system, he could hardly make himself clearer:

> Y cuando he de escribir una comedia,
> Encierro los preceptos con seis llaves;
> Saco a Terencio y Plauto de mi estudio,
> Para que no me den voces; que suele
> Dar gritos la verdad en libros mudos;
> Y escribo por el arte que inventaron
> Los que el vulgar aplauso pretendieron;
> Porque, como las paga el vulgo, es justo
> Hablarle en necio para darle gusto.

Over the years the part of the poem that deals with Lope's manner of writing plays has been considered by critics in various ways, among others, by Ticknor: "Lope took the theatre in the state in which he found it; and instead of attempting to adapt it to any previous theory, or to any existing models, whether ancient or recent, made it his great object to satisfy the popular audiences of his age";[3] by Morel-Fabio: "il ne réclame rien, il a suivi le

---

[2] In a note to me Bruce Wardropper makes this comment: "I would myself be more inclined to think (with Menéndez Pidal!) that Lope is being ironic. Is he not saying in effect: 'You fellows, *students* of dramatic theory, think you know all there is to writing plays. I, as a mere *practitioner* of the art, know nothing, of course.' Irony, if my reading is correct, is anything but polite."

[3] George Ticknor, *History of Spanish Literature* (Boston, 1863), II, 177.

courant, voilà tout;[4] by Fitzmaurice-Kelly: "what takes the form of an apology is in truth a vaunt";[5] by Menéndez y Pelayo: "una lamentable palinodia que apenas es menester citar porque vive en la memoria de todos";[6] by Rennert y Castro: "una defensa de las irregularidades de sus comedias y de la inobservancia de las reglas clásicas";[7] by Menéndez Pidal: "la expresión irónica ... de los principios artísticos concebidos por Lope en su primera juventud";[8] by Northup and Adams, "Lope in hangdog and cynical fashion admits himself a money-making sinner. ... *El arte nuevo* is a plea of confession and avoidance."[9]

Is Lope's statement about writing for the public to be taken seriously? For my part, I think it should be, keeping in mind Lope's experience with the theater, rather than what he may have read about the unities, and all that. If we believe Lope here, and I think we should, what he says is this, that it is the public that determines the character of his plays. This is what is new in the art of Lope.

In a recent article in the *Revista de Occidente* José F. Montesinos writes: "Si Lope hace lo que hace no es por ignorancia; es porque tiene que hacerlo. Conste que lo que le lleva a hacerlo no es la ignorancia de la poética; la poética la tenía él en la uña desde la infancia. Es que tiene que vivir, y tiene que vivir de algo que desconocen humanistas y señores, de algo enteramente nuevo, exigente, imperioso, violento a veces: el público."[10]

Montesinos' phrase "tiene que vivir" deserves particular attention. Financial support by patrons was not uncommon in those days

---

[4] Alfred Morel-Fatio, *La* Comedia *espagnole du XVII⁰ siècle* (Paris, 1885), p. 31.

[5] James Fitzmaurice-Kelly, *History of Spanish Literature* (New York, 1910), p. 255.

[6] Marcelino Menéndez y Pelayo, *Historia de las ideas estéticas en España* (Madrid, 1907-20), III (1920), 433.

[7] Hugo A. Rennert, y Américo Castro, *Vida de Lope de Vega* (Madrid, 1919), p. 187.

[8] Ramón Menéndez Pidal, "Lope de Vega: 'El Arte nuevo' y la nueva biografía," *RFE*, XXII (1935), 352.

[9] George Tyler Northup, *An Introduction to Spanish Literature* (Chicago, 1925), p. 271; 3rd ed., revised and enlarged by Nicholson B. Adams (Chicago, 1960), p. 272.

[10] "La paradoja del 'Arte nuevo'," *Rev. de Occidente*, Año II, 2.ª época (1964), p. 314.

and certainly was not something to be despised, as every writer of the time knew very well indeed. But this type of support could not be counted on with any degree of certainty. It depended too much on the whim of the patron. He might not be feeling at his best, he might be short of ready money, he might even be cross with his mistress for having done him wrong. In short, at the moment he might not be in the mood for dealing out anything at all—and hard money was urgently needed by the author.

If the author wrote a book, there were numerous obstacles that stood in the way of cash. The author must get a "licencia" from the Consejo de la Cámara, which arranged for one or two censors who presumably knew something about the subject. These censors were probably in no hurry to carry out their task. And this is quite understandable, for apparently they were not paid for their work. The Santo Oficio de la Inquisición must then approve. It might expurgate, or even condemn the book to the fire. Next, the "privilegio" must be secured from the Consejo. This was something like the copyright of today. Then, an ecclesiastical "licencia" had to be secured, though this was sometimes evaded (there is none in the first edition of the *Quijote*).

And last, but certainly not least, money must be forthcoming to get the book printed. Sometimes this was offered by the patron in return for complimentary remarks ("dedicatoria") in the opening pages. Or the "privilegio" might be sold outright to the printer, who would then have exclusive rights to the book.[11] The contract for printing was a little complicated. It included an agreement on the kind of paper to be used, number of copies to be printed, the total cost, how soon to start printing and how long it would take. The official corrector was appointed by the Consejo de la Cámara. He was to read the proof and check the printed version against the censored manuscript. Right along here the author would probably secure a number of "composicions lauditorias" from friends who liked to see their names in print. And finally, a sale price (*tasa*) for each copy was set officially at so much a signature (*pliego*).[12]

---

[11] In the introduction to *Ocho comedias* Cervantes writes: "Vendíselas al tal librero... él me las pagó razonablemente, yo cogí mi dinero con suavedad sin tener cuenta con dimes ni diretes de recitantes."

[12] A. G. de Amezúa y Mayo, "Como se hacía un libro en nuestro siglo de oro," in *Opúsculos histórico-literarios* (Madrid, 1951), I, 331-373.

Guillermo de Torre has pointed out the poverty of Lope,[13] and explained how little he — or any other writer of his time — could rely on financial assistance from a patron, or make much money from any book or articles that he might publish: "Para llegar a encontrar un escritor que viva estrictamente de su pluma no sólo con holgura, sino hasta cierto lujo, llegando a cobrar por sus artículos cantidades superiores a las que entonces había percibido ningún otro, hay que avanzar hasta el primer tercio del siglo XIX y llegar al en un todo excepcional Larra."

Capitalizing on a *comedia* was quite different from trying to do it with a book. The dramatist could sell his play direct to the manager of the theatrical company, the *autor de comedias*, as he was called. The dramatist received immediate payment and the deal was closed. A few bills could now be paid. Of course, the manager of the company would have to deal with the censor, but that was his headache, not the author's.

We must remember that the price received for plays was not inconsiderable. For example, we know that Lope received as much as 500 reales for some of his plays. However, this sum, 500 reales, does not mean anything unless we translate it into commodities.

And here is where the researcher runs into difficulties. There are innumerable books on the economy of Spain, and they give many pictures of Spanish coins, and other details of this sort. But as to what the money was really worth in terms of commodities, these books remain silent. However, some indication of prices in those times is available. In his *Spain in Decline* R. Trevor Davies quotes from a letter written by the new English ambassador in Madrid, Sir Arthur Hopton, who had been informed that his allowance for maintenance had been reduced from five pounds a day to four. Naturally, Sir Arthur protested: "All the diet of table and stables is three times as dear as in Sir Charles Cornwallis' time, when two pounds a day was first added. A loaf of bread was then worth 12 *maravedís* and it is now worth 34. An azumbre ... of wine was then

---

[13] "Lope de Vega y la condición económico-social del escritor en el siglo XVII," *CHA*, Nos. 161-162 (May-June, 1963), 249-261. Rennert and Castro (*Vida de Lope de Vega*, Ch. xiii) dwell at length on the poverty of Lope.

worth 12 *maravedís,* and now sells for 30 ; a pound of mutton, which was then worth 17 *maravedís,* is now worth 40." [14]

Let us see what one could buy for 500 reales from 1605 to 1609, when Sir Charles Cornwallis was ambassador in Madrid. There were 34 *maravedís* in a real, and 500 reales equal 17,000 *maravedís.* If we divide this number by 12, the price of a loaf of bread, we get 1400 loaves of bread. Continuing with the mathematics, and changing the *azumbre* to English quarts (about two to an *azumbre*), we get around 2800 quarts of wine. By the same process we get 1000 pounds of mutton in 1605-09. In summary, is a play were sold for 500 reales, it would buy 1400 loaves of bread, or 2800 quarts (not fifths) of wine, or 1000 pounds of mutton.

One disturbing thought in this calculation of the cost of living in Spain at this time is the possibility that Sir Arthur may have been exaggerating in order to get his per diem raised. Another possibility is that the Spaniards over-charged the English representatives, who

---

[14] R. Trevor Davies, *Spain in Decline, 1621-1700* (London, 1957), p. 104. These figures do not quite agree with Earl J. Hamilton, *American Treasure and the Price Revolution in Spain, 1501-1650* (Cambridge, Mass., 1934), p. 370. He gives mutton at 26 maravedís a pound in 1605, and wine at 173.8 an arroba (8 azumbres) in 1605. Casiano Pellicer quotes a statement made in 1614 by one of the hospitals in Madrid: "[el pan] se había subido de tres quartos y medio a seis: el carnero de cinco y medio a siete y medio," *Tratado histórico...,* p. 160. Can this be as much as 51 maravedís for bread, and 65 maravedís for mutton?

Bruce Wardropper has called my attention to a statement by W. Somerset Maugham: "[Lope's] main source of livelihood was his pen. The managers paid fifty ducats for a play. A ducat was worth five shillings, but so far as I can make out its purchasing power was about equal to that of a pound. Since this does not mean very much I have had the curiosity to note the relative prices that were paid for certain commodities. According to the contriver in Cervantes' *Coloquio de Cipión y Berganza* a man could live on a real and a half a day, and there were eleven reales in a ducat. From *La Gitanilla* I gather then ten ducats was a good price to pay for a donkey; fifty, as I have just said, for a three act play; and when Cervantes was rescued from slavery in Algiers his ranson was five hundred. On the other hand when a middle-aged gentleman desired to be rid of Cervantes' daughter, who had been living under his protection, he had to provide her with a house and two thousand ducats. From this it is evident that a play was worth ten times as much as a donkey and a man of genius fifty times; but a maiden's innocence was worth more than four times as much as a man of genius. The price of a virtuous woman, as we know, is far above rubies." *Don Fernando, or Variations on Some Spanish Themes* (Garden City, N. Y., 1935), p. 152.

were not altogether popular in Spain in this period. But, laying these problems aside, and making some allowance for possible exaggeration, we may conclude that if an author sold a play for 500 reales, he came into possesion of considerable purchasing power. Writing saleable plays was good business.

It is not to be supposed that all the authors received the same recompense for their plays that Lope did, but we may well surmise that they made enough to keep alive and even secure some "fringe benefits."

The public of those days was evidently just as enthusiastic about plays as some people are today about the movies. They wanted something new all the time. The result was a very considerable demand. And the writers endeavored to keep up with it. They could see that there was "Gold in them thar hills."

If the plays were items intended for sale, they would have to be saleable, that is, acceptable to the manager of the company. Is it not, therefore, likely that the writer in question would take into account the kind of play he had sold to the impresario previously, and try to write another more or less like it? What was the sense of experimenting? He nedeed money. He had to live.

And he was not the only one. How about the manager of the company that was to put the play on? For one thing, he was not likely to pay good money for a play unless he had reason to think that he could get a satisfactory return from its presentation on the stage. And another thing — the problem of success with the public was not his only concern. In his company he undoubtedly had an actress who was something of a prima donna. She would not be modest in her demands, nor would she be peaceful in her conduct if she did not get what she wanted. And she probably had certain conditions spelled out. Pérez Pastor gives us information about contracts in which the principal actress is guaranteed either all the principal parts, or some of the principal parts, and no less than secondary parts. [15] In view of such demands we can be fairly sure

---

[15] Cristóbal Pérez Pastor, *Nuevos datos acerca del histrionismo español en los siglos XVI y XVII* (Madrid, 1901), and "Nuevos datos acerca del histrionismo español en los siglos XVI y XVII. Segunda serie," *BH*, XIV (1902), 300-317. Here are some of these contracts: 1632. Obligación de María Calderón, de ir a la villa de Pinto... haciendo los primeros papeles... *Nuevos datos*, p. 226. 1636. Obligación de Francisco Maire y su mujer Jacinta Vélez

that if the principal actress did not have a good role assigned to her, she would refuse to play, or, if she did, would do it badly and be disagreeable about it. The life of the manager was not always a happy one.

And so the author, in putting the play together, and making it saleable, had to consider the manager of the company, the public, the members of the dramatic company, and especially the principal actress. It was quite a large order, but he had to live.

Thornton Wilder, who is not as well-known as he should be as an authority on the plays of Lope de Vega, gives some testimony along the lines that we are pursuing. In an article entitled "Lope, Pinedo, some Child Actors and a Lion," [16] he explains how Baltasar Pinedo and his wife played the principal roles in the company of Gaspar de Porras (or Porres). Pinedo was not young, but he was admirable in scenes of frenzy and in lamentations. Juana, his wife, was a *mujer varonil*, an Amazon type of woman. Wilder gives examples of plays that Lope wrote with them in mind, plays with characters suited to the special talents of this interesting couple. There were children in the company, and Lope has children in these plays, and as the children grow up, the parts they play are fixed to correspond with their ages. Wilder is not sure whether the lion was real, or whether he was a man in a lion's skin, but in any case he must have been something of a sensation, and a drawing card for the play.

An examination of the plays mentioned by Wilder makes it abundantly clear that Lope shaped a number of his plays to fit the

---

de ir a la villa de Algete para ayudar a representar dos comedias... haciendo Jacinta la primera parte en las representaciones y cantar y bailar... *Nuevos datos*, p. 247. 1637. Concierto de María de Quiñones... durante un año para representar todos los papeles principales de dama... *Nuevos datos*, p. 258. 1639. Obligación de Francisca Paula Pérez... durante un año, para hacer todos los principales papeles y cantar y bailar... *Nuevos datos*, p. 303. 1641. Obligación de Isabel María, mujer soltera, de asistir en la compañía de Antonio de Rueda durante un año para hacer los principales papeles o segundos de dama, y no menos... *BH*, XIV, p. 309. And this was not the whole story of the demands of the actresses. It seems to have been fairly common for these high-strung ladies to insist upon having two horses available for them when the company was on the road. They had no intention of travelling in the baggage car. And in one contract the manager agrees to get a trunk out of hock in order to coax the lady to sign on the dotted line.

[16] *RPh*, VII (1953), 19-26.

company that was to put them on.[17] Was he the only one to do this? Unfortunately, we know so little about the actual presentation of plays of the Golden Age that unassailable evidence that this was a general practice is lacking. But, at all events, it seems very likely.

If the principal actress was temperamental — and no doubt she was — one of the most important considerations in writing a play was, of course, a good role for her. If the play had this, there would be an excellent chance that the manager would buy the manuscript. He could be pretty sure that it would be a success with the public. At any rate, the touchy actress would not make trouble.

Let us see, then, if there is any evidence in the *comedias* to support the supposition that the role of the principal actress was all important. In the first place, we can name a considerable number of plays by Lope and others which appear to have been constructed with some particular actress in mind, plays in which the principal character is a woman around whom most of the action centers. There is Lope's *Una noche toledana*, in which a girl sets a whole hotel in tumult by making dates for men to come to her room at night, dates which she has no intention of keeping. The audience doesn't know this and looks forward to considerable excitement in the girl's room. There is excitement in her room all right, but not of the kind expected.

Tirso's *La prudencia en la mujer* deals with the ways in which a woman circumvents the intrigues of a swarm of unscrupulous courtiers. Alarcón's *Las paredes oyen* has as its principal character Doña Ana, who is successful in warding off a too enthusiastic suitor and in winning another hand, that of a bashful lover whom she prefers. Calderón's *La dama duende* is all about an ingenious lady who bedevils a man lodged in an adjoining room. A list of plays of this type could be extended almost indefinitely.

One is tempted to bring in Lope's *Fuenteovejuna* as an example of an author's desire to insure the cooperation of the principal actress. In this play the whole town is the protagonist when it rises in wild fury to avenge the wrongs done by the overlord, the Comendador. In this mass of people, one stands out, a country girl,

---

[17] Rennert and Castro mention only one play, *La dama boba*, that Lope wrote for a specific actress, Jerónima de Burgos (*Vida de Lope*, pp. 176-177, 217, 259).

Laurencia. In the first act she is disdainful, rather cold, in fact. She has a fairly long speech about her love of simple life, a rather boring one (and really out of character) when she makes an elaborate play on words, she has a refusal of the attentions of the Comendador, and a reasonable number of other appearances. But there isn't much to set her above the other characters. There is little chance for emotion to be expressed. There is no big moment.

Lope, however, has one in store. This is in Act II, when the city fathers are debating what to do about the wicked deeds of the Comendador. Into the group rushes Laurencia, *desmelenada* (her hair and clothes in disarray). She tells her father not to call her daughter any more, and then she turns of the men. She has been raped by the Comendador. If the men do nothing to avenge this and other wrongs done by him, they are "cobardes, pastores, ovejas, liebres, gallinas, hilanderas, maricones." They should be wearing women's clothes. They are not men, they are "medio-hombres." Her words set the group on fire. Something must be done. And it is done. The Comendador is brutally murdered.

If we recall the actions of the rabble-rouser La Pasionaria in the Spanish Civil War,[18] we may come to the conclusion that the appearance of Laurencia before the city authorities has had its counterpart in real life. And yet, when we consider the length of Laurencia's speech and the crudeness of her language, we are forced to conclude that Lope had the actress, even some special actress, in mind when he came to this point in the play. He wanted to give her one supreme moment, and he surely succeeded in pleasing her — and the manager.

There are plays in which it seems that the part of the actress has been padded, so that she will have at least one scene in which she can show great emotion and get the undivided attention of the audience in an impressive way. It isn't always easy for the author

---

[18] "The rallying cry of El Caudillo's opponents was 'No pasarán.' First to use the war cry was the foremost woman Communist of the time, La Pasionaria, Basque-born Dolores Ibarruri, whose fiery orations urging women to fight Franco 'with knives and burning oil' made world headlines. Today, at 66, she lives in exile here [Moscow], is always present at Red rallies. She also delivers four or five anti-Franco broadcasts weekly over Radio Moscow and Radio Prague. Each ends, in hoary Red tradition, 'Workers of the World, Unite'," *Newsweek*, 2 July 1962, p. 10.

to do this without sacrificing logic and probability. But it has to be done, to keep the actress satisfied. We will cite some examples.

In Act I of Lope's *El remedio en la desdicha* the actress who has the principal feminine role, that of Jarifa, appears as a sweet, gentle, modest lady. She has little emotion to express, and what she has, she covers up. She doesn't appear at all in Act II. Will the high-strung actress be content with a part like this? Hardly. So Lope proceeds to make up for it in Act III. Here, Jarifa and her sweetheart Abindarráez are united after a sad separation. In Act II Abindarráez has been captured by the Spanish Captain and almost misses his tremendously important date with Jarifa. Indeed, he would have, had not the Spanish Captain released him on parole. In Act III Abindarráez appears at the house of Jarifa, who makes it abundantly clear that she is glad to see him. She shares her bed with him. (These pleasant moments take place offstage.) The next morning (this is onstage), she finds Abindarráez sad, moaning around, seemingly in very low spirits. Thereupon, she turns loose in a passionate speech — and a fairly long one it is — calling him "ingrato," "esquivo," "cruel," "el más villano del suelo." He has found her unsatisfactory, she says. He is like all men who have had their way with women. He should clear out, unjust tyrant that he is, and depart with his pleasure and her dishonor. She will kill herself.

Abindarráez listens to all this rather mournfully. He cannot get in a word — her reproaches come in such a tumult. But when she is about to carry out her threat, he has a chance to speak up and tell her that he truly loves her. The reason for his seemingly ungrateful attitude, he says, is that when he was on his way to meet her, he was badly wounded by the Spanish Captain in no less than three places, "en brazo, muslo y espaldas." This seems all to the good, and Jarifa is happy. She says so. Here is a good chance for the actress to register another kind of emotion, to show that she can change her style from fire and fury to sweetness and love. But — if we reconstruct the situation, we must ask this question, how could Jarifa have slept with Abindarráez all night, and not found out about at least some of his wounds? The answer is not forthcoming. Lope has got himself into a blind alley. He had to, to keep the actress in good humor, and convince her that the role of Jarifa was a good one.

If we turn to Calderón's *El alcalde de Zalamea*, we find examples of 1) consideration for a comic actor in the company, 2) a keen concern for the reaction of the audience, and 3) an unreasonable extension of the role of the principal actress.

In the first act of this play there is a tiresome *hidalgo*, Don Mendo, who with his servant indulges in a few jokes that are supposed to be funny. They were taken in part from the picaresque novel, *Lazarillo de Tormes*, where the humor is, to be sure, pretty grim, but it is humor just the same. In Calderón's play this odd character, Don Mendo, appears for quite a while in Act I, only briefly in Act II, and fortunately not at all in Act III. He is not necessary to the action in any way.[19] He is what the Spaniards call a "zero on the left." Why is he in the play at all? The only apparent explanation is that there was a comic actor in the company and it seemed like a good idea at the time to give him something to do. The part of Don Mendo contributed little to the play, but maybe the comic actor was conciliated.

In the third act of his play we have a scene which most critics consider a masterpiece, the best thing that Calderón ever did. Here Pedro Crespo begs the Captain, who has violated Crespo's daughter, to right the wrong by marrying the girl. Pedro lays aside the staff of office that gives him authority as mayor, and speaks to the Captain as a private citizen. He begs him by all that is holy to do the right thing. He offers the Captain all his property, says he will sell himself and his son into slavery, and even kneels down before him with tears in his eyes, entreating him to marry Isabel, the girl in question.

At first sight, this looks all right, but the point is that if the Captain refuses, Pedro Crespo as mayor has no jurisdiction in the case. Legally, the Captain should be tried by a military court. Pedro Crespo knows this — and the Captain tells him so in no uncertain terms. Not only this, but Pedro Crespo can see from the

---

[19] In the comment to the recording of this play by RCA Española, we find the following: "En esta [versión] se respeta casi enteramente el original, sustituyendo algunas palabras y conceptos, y se suprimen los personajes del hidalgo Don Mendo y su criado Nuño, por considerar que su intervención, ajena a la línea directa del drama, es menos comprensible si no se pueden ver sus dos figuras, trasunto de las de Don Quijote y su escudero Sancho Panza."

very outset that the Captain will absolutely reject any offer that he may make. Pedro Crespo can offer the Captain the proverbial pie in the sky. Anyone can offer anybody anything, if he knows the offer will not be accepted. This is the case with Pedro Crespo. But we must admit that the actor who plays this part has some good lines.

Why is this scene there? The audience must be "conditioned" to accept without protest the death of an officer in the King's army at the hands of a civilian, as happens at the end of the play. To be doubly sure that the audience reacts in the proper way, Calderón has the King happen along at the right moment and, before anyone in the audience can frame an objection to the murder, for that it is, the King gives his approval of the execution. If the King thinks it is all right, who in the audience can find fault? [20]

The actress who plays the part of Isabel has little to do in the first two acts, where she appears as a modest girl, with few pretensions, obedient to her father. Surely, if she continues in this way for the rest of the play, the role will not be very acceptable. How can the actress, who is proud, jealous, and ambitious, consent to have the three actors who play the parts of Pedro Crespo, the Captain, and the General (an extremely good role) get the best lines — and the most applause? The solution is simple: give the proud beauty a considerable number of good lines, even though it is contrary to common sense. In Act III Isabel could relate the sad story of her violation in four words, certainly in four lines, but Calderón has her tell her story twice and in great detail, once in 67 lines of soliloquy, and again in 174 lines, when she tells her father what has happened. Even the most demanding actress must admit that these two speeches are worth waiting for.

The question of the influence of the public on the plays of the Golden Age becomes complicated with the ascent to the throne of Philip IV in 1621. Philip had a great interest in the theater and had many plays performed at his court. There is no way of telling what plays were presented at court except for some that are clearly

---

[20] See "Pedro Crespo and the Captain in Calderón's *Alcalde de Zalamea*," *infra*, pp. 118-119. Bruce Wardropper in a personal note, says: "He [Pedro Crespo] appeals for a gentlemanliness which he knows will not be forthcoming because he must exhaust all possibilities of a lawful peaceable solution before taking the law into his own hands."

"spectaculars," written expressly for Philip IV. We may surmise, however, that after 1621 writers had a twofold purpose: to please the public in the city, and also the spectators at court. We do not know what reward the manager of the company or the actors received for performances before the King, but certainly it was not something to be despised, even if it consisted only of publicity and prestige.

But the question as to what was the taste of the King and his courtiers remains unanswered. One possible clue may be found in the famous play *La vida es sueño*. According to Vera Tassis, who published Calderón's plays after his death, this *comedia* was a "Fiesta que sè representó a sus Majestades en el Salón de su Real Palacio." Some people sneer at Vera Tassis, and question his veracity, but he may have been right this time. At any rate, the language of the play seems hardly suited to the rough and ready audience downtown. Who of this *hoi polloi* could possibly know what a hippogriff was, mentioned in the very first line, and who Phaeton was a few lines further on? Calderón here, and indeed throughout the play, is trying hard to write in a lofty style. To me this play shows signs of having been written "on order" from the Court, and with too little time before the deadline.

Just what happened to a *comedia* after it passed into the hands of the manager of the company is not known, but we can make a few reasonable conjectures. The manager had to submit it to a censor, if he had not already done so before buying it. The censor might object to some of the lines and insist on deleting them. The manager, no doubt, modified the manuscript to make an acting copy, changing and omitting lines as he pleased. It was, after all, his property. It would be passed from hand to hand among the members of the company, and somebody would copy off the parts. It would be stored away, probably without great concern, when not needed, and carried around on tour. After a while it would be in pretty bad shape, "manoseado," as Cervantes would say.

In Parte IV of Lope's plays, the editor, Gaspar de Porres, speaks of "Los agravios que muchas personas hacen cada día al autor de este libro, imprimiendo sus comedias tan bárbaras como las han hallado después de muchos años que salieron de sus manos, donde apenas hay cosa concertada, y los que padece de otros que por sus particulares intereses imprimen o representan las que no son suyas con su nombre."[21] After all, these "muchas personas" had to live.

During the months and years of passing from hand to hand, the play might have been worn out, or lost altogether. If the author wanted the play back, how did he get it? And how much did he have to pay for it? This we do not know.

And here it is interesting to note that eight "Partes" of the plays of Lope de Vega were published between 1604 and 1617 before he ventured to take the credit for putting them in print. Rennert and Castro, in their life of Lope de Vega, have serious doubts that these eight parts were printed without his authorization. This seems not only doubtful but most unlikely.

No doubt Lope did instigate the printing of these eight "Partes," but apparently he felt that he needed a smoke screen. He did not want to be visible in the picture, in case authorizing the publication of such ordinary things as plays were criticized. And when he does acknowledge that he is printing them he makes excuses. In Parte IX he says: "Viendo imprimir cada día mis comedias de suerte que era imposible llamarlas mías... me he resuelto a imprimirlas por mis originales; que aunque es verdad que no las escribí con este ánimo, ni para que de los oídos del teatro se trasladaran a la censura de los aposentos."[22] And Lope is not the only one to be reluctant to claim credit for plays in print. Can it be that dramatists of his time felt that it was undignified, unseemly, or even unworthy of them to publish pieces that had been dashed off to make a little quick money, plays that could not compare with respectable compositions like epic poems, and other ambitious efforts? For my part, I can see no reason for this false modesty other than that the *comedias* were looked upon as merchandise, and after the manager of the company had finished with them, they were shopworn, and little to be proud of.

Writing plays to make money was not confined to the Golden Age in Spain. It happened everywhere — it happens now. It is good business, if the dramatist is successful. And we may be fairly sure that when the dramatist of the Golden Age was writing a play, he, Lope and others of that time, had well in mind the possible reaction

---

[21] Rennert y Castro, *Vida de Lope de Vega*, p. 222.
[22] *Ibid.*, p. 261.

of the public. This respect for the public is not new in the entertainment world, but it is unusual for it to be considered in the world of scholarship. It is hardly thought of in dealing with the plays of the Golden Age, but it surely needs to be taken into account in studying and judging the *comedias* of that period.

One final word. Let it be made crystal clear that the writer of this article would not for a moment deny the dramatic and literary values in the plays of the Golden Age in Spain. Rather the wonder is that these plays have so much merit, written, as they were, to sell, to get some quick money. They were pot boilers. The dramatists had to live.

PMLA, LXXXII (1967), 178-184.

Chapter III

LIONS IN EARLY SPANISH LITERATURE AND ON THE
SPANISH STAGE

Before venturing into the den of lions which lies ahead, it may be well to make the acquaintance of a few varmints that appear for a brief moment on the Spanish stage, and then are seen no more.

Lope de Vega has a bear in *El casamiento en la muerte,* and another in *Alejandro el Segundo,* both of which are disposed of without difficulty. A tiger appears in Tirso's *Escarmientos para el cuerdo* and seizes the *gracioso* Diagnito, but does no apparent harm. A number of serpents make themselves heard in the wings of the Spanish stage and their hissing invariably proves to be bad luck, bad luck for them, because they soon get their heads cut off. We see the bloody heads, but seldom the serpents. In Lope's *El amor enamorado* and in *Perseo,* however, the serpents actually appear on the stage, "echando fuego." In *El vellocino de oro* we have quite a menagerie. There is Pegasus, with wings; there is a dragon which guards the Golden Fleece; and there are two bulls which breathe out fire.

In *Fortunas de Andrómeda y Perseo,* Calderón presents a hydra with seven heads and a dog with three, but these outlandish creatures do little more than mildly frighten the *gracioso*. In the same play we have a monster all covered with scales, who, when wounded by Perseus, jumps into the sea and drowns. Best of all in this play is Medusa "vestida de pieles," her head bristling with snakes. Perseus chases this attractive female off the stage, and then on again. The second time he cuts off her head before our eyes. Not only this, but he accidentally drops the head, and to our surprise—and probably to the surprise of Perseus as well—the head bounces!

The lions in early Spanish literature and on the Spanish stage are usually friendly, although the first one that comes to mind, the lion in the *Poema del Cid,* scares the daylights out of the Infantes de Carrión. But the Cid takes him by the scruff of his neck and puts him right back in his cage.

The next lion also appears in a poem, *La vida de Santa María Egipciaca.* When María comes to the end of her adventurous days and dies in the desert, the hermit who finds her has no tools with which to dig her grave, and the ground is hard as rock. Whereupon, a lion comes down from a mountain and helps him excavate. Later, the lion assists the hermit in filling in the grave. The Spanish version of the burial of this interesting lady is tame, indeed, as compared with its French source. In Robert Grosseteste's *Vie de Sainte Marie l'Egyptienne* the lion digs the grave all by himself after the hermit had given him the measurements. Then the hermit takes hold of Marie's shoulders and the lion takes her feet, and the two of them lower the body into the grave. After this, the lion puts the earth back, kneels on the ground, makes a sign that he will leave, and does just that. What more could any lion have done, at any time, or at any place?

In the first romance of chivalry, *El Caballero Zifar,* while the Caballero is taking a little nap after lunch, a lioness carries off the older of his two children. The kidnapping turns out to be quite unimportant, however, because the boy is soon rescued.

In a later romance of chivalry, *Palmerín de Inglaterra,* the noble lady Flérida gives birth to twin sons in a wood, and shortly thereafter a savage, who lives in that region, comes along with two lions on a leash. That was the way he hunted. It had been a bad day for game, though, and the lions had caught nothing. When the savage sees the babies, quite naturally it occurs to him that they would make good eating for his lions. He does not feed the babies to them right away, however, but carries them home, where his wife finds some other food for the hungry animals. Time passes and the children get to be big boys of eight or nine. They become mighty hunters, one of them especially, Floriano, "en cuya compañía los leones siempre andaban." One day when the boy was out hunting, he sicked the lions on a deer, lost sight of the lions, and got lost himself. He was picked up by a *caballero* who took the boy to his (Floriano's) own mother. Meantime, the lions had killed the deer and got all bloody doing it. When they returned home without Floriano, the savage, thinking that they had killed the boy, killed them. They deserved a better fate. Later in the novel Palmerín encounters two lions and two tigers, all of which are disposed of in summary fashion.

In one of the imitations of the *Celestina*, the *Tragedia Policiana* by Sebastián Fernández, the author has a lion take the life of the hero, rather than have the hero fall off the wall, as is the case in the more famous novel. Here is how is happened. In Act 26 of this very dull story, a lion is let loose in the garden to scare away some foxes. The young lover Policiano (almost the exact counterpart of Calisto in the *Celestina*) goes with his servants to "gozar de los amores de Philomena," and climbs up a ladder (just as in the *Celestina*) to do so. He does not find the girl, but the lion finds him. Policiano is torn to pieces, and later on, Philomena is found "bañada en sangre," evidently a suicide.

The first lion to appear on the Spanish stage, it seems, is introduced by Cervantes. In *El trato de Argel*, a Christian captive, trying to escape from the Moors, gets lost and hides in some bushes, after calling on the Virgin to send him a ransom. The Christian goes to sleep, and who should come along but a lion, who lies down beside him, "muy manso." In due time, the lion guides the pious Christian to safety.—Before we take leave of Cervantes, we must not forget the sleepy lion in the second part of the *Quixote*.

Thornton Wilder has an article in *Romance Philology* (VII, 19-25) entitled "Lope, Pinedo, Some Child Actors and a Lion," in which he advances the idea that the theatrical manager, Baltasar de Pinedo, "for a year or two was in possession of a lion or a costume made from a lion skin." Mr. Wilder mentions three plays of Lope in which this lion appears: *La varona castellana*, *La serrana de la Verá*, and *Los palacios de Galiana*. Mr. Wilder was inclined to think that Pinedo "enjoyed the services of a poor, aged and edentate beast, simply because the lion is always called upon to do the same thing—to come to the feet of a leading actor and lie down."

Thornton Wilder goes on to say that another manager, Melchor de Villalba, also "had a lion or a lion's skin some five years earlier, and Lope wrote several plays for its appearance, including one on the subject of Androcles and the lion, *El esclavo de Roma*. There, too, Thornton Wilder says, "The animal is merely required to subside at Androcles' feet with a show of affection and gratitude." It must be said that in this otherwise uninteresting play the lion has considerably more to do than Thornton Wilder indicates. In the second act Andronio (Androcles) befriends the lion by taking a piece of arrow from its paw. In the third act the lion makes two appearances. In the first of these scenes the lion brings Andronio a *conejo,* and in the second the lion, who, as we know, is supposed to eat Andronio for the enjoyment of the Emperor and his fun-loving pals, stops on seeing Andronio, shows him the paw that had been wounded, and the two, Andronio and the lion, embrace. This nice lion, as we see, has quite an important role.

Thornton Wilder does not tell us what other plays Lope wrote for Melchor de Villalba, but one of them might have been *El hijo de Reduán.* In this play a lion gets out of its cage and scares everyone but the hero Gomel, who has been brought up in the wilds and is well acquainted with wild beasts and their ways. Gomel faces the animal resolutely and wonders if this is not a lion that was a friend of his in his youth. Gomel speaks kindly to him:

¡Oh, buen amigo! ¿qué hay?
¿Cómo va? ¿Qué es menester?"

The attitude of the animal makes Gomel say, aside:

¡Por Dios, que es cosa de ver
El regocijo que tray.

Gomel then greets his friend in a most affectionate way, and says:

¡Dame uno y mil abrazos.

Gomel thinks this lion is a good omen, and it really is. Gomel goes to sleep on the throne, and the lion lies down at his feet. People come in and in their amazement decide that a man like this is worthy to be king. They make him one.

In Lope's *Adonis y Venus* there are two lions, but all they do is to come out of a temple at the end of the play and throw themselves at the feet of Venus. The title of Lope's *El hijo de los leones* gives promise of quite an extended part for one lion or more, but the lion's actions are, for the most part, narrated. It is quite a story, though, and might well be called "Lady Fenisa's Lover." Lady Fenisa has an illegitimate son by her lover, who is no ordinary grounds keeper, but the son of the King of Alexandria. Wishing to keep her shame a secret, Fenisa takes the baby into the woods where she thinks the wild beasts may eat it. Strangely enough, this never seems to happen in such cases. A hermit, Fileno, lives in the vicinity, and some time before, he had found a lioness with her foot caught in a trap. The hermit, of course, had released the lioness, who thereupon became his friend. One day, greatly to the hermit's surprise, the animal brings in a baby in a basket. The lioness suckles this baby for a year and a half, and the baby thrives on the high voltage diet. The child grows up with wild animals and acts so much like them that the peasants think he is a monster. Quite appropriately, the boy has been named Leonido. Lisardo, the father of the boy, goes out to kill the "monster" that had been reported to him. He finds him asleep and is about to slay him when: "Sale un león y despierta a Leonido." Of course, father and son become friends, and eventually marriage makes everything right. We are not informed whether the lion was invited to the wedding.

In Lope's *El Cardenal de Belén* the lion has quite an extensive part. In the first act it is related how "una fiera leona" saved San Jerónimo from a Moor who pursued him into a cave. In the third act, when Jerónimo is preaching a sermon, lo and behold, a lion dashes in and interrupts the service. The lion shows Jerónimo his "mano." Jerónimo talks kindly to him:

> Espera, amigo león,
> ¿Qué tienes? ¿De qué te quejas?

Right away Jerónimo sees what is wrong. He takes a thorn out of the lion's paw and the lion kisses his feet in gratitude. (This is the Androcles story so far, but the rest is different.) Later, the *gracioso*, Marino, comes in with the lion and a donkey. Marino tells the donkey the story of the lion and informs the lion that his duty is to take the donkey out to pasture and keep the wild beasts away from him. The lion evidently thinks this is all right, for he nods assent. Shortly after this the *gracioso* comes in, "azotando el león." Why is this? It seems that the lion has failed in his duty

—the donkey has been eaten by wild animals, or stolen. To this serious accusation the lion solemnly shakes his head. No, it isn't so. Thereupon, Merino tells the lion to go find the donkey, or be faced with the prospect of not having anything to eat for four days. After a while, three Jews appear, pursued by the lion. They explain that they found the donkey, but no one was around except a lion asleep under a tree. They thought the donkey did not belong to anyone, so they took it. When the lion hears this phony story, he tries to attack the three "hebreos," but Marino holds him back. At the end of the play there is a tableau in which San Jerónimo appears with the lion beside him. This lion richly deserves recognition.

Among the plays of doubtful authorship, and attributed in some editions to Lope de Vega, is *La mayor dicha en el monte,* dealing with life of San Eustaquio. According to legend this saint and his family were thrown into a lion's den and the lions did not attack them. Thereupon, the emperor had to dream up another way to put them to death. Early in the play a lion comes on stage and carries off one of Eustaquio's two children. A bear (not seen on the stage) carries off the other. At the end of the play the whole family of San Eustaquio is thrown into a den of lions. The stage directions say: "salen dos leones y salen al encuentro los hijos; y ellos se echan a los pies." Trajan is amazed—and no wonder— for the lions act like puppies, even though one of the two boys is foolish enough to try to provoke them to action.

Tirso de Molina seems to have had no use for lions, except, in one play, *La fingida Acadia,* and that play merely presents a lion painted on a canvas.

In one of his earliest plays Guillén de Castro has a lion who merely makes his entrance and scares the Infanta. The hero Leonido comes in with his sword drawn, chases the lion off stage, and the Infanta describes the killing.

In a later work, *Las maravillas de Babilonia,* Guillén de Castro really outdoes himself—and his contemporaries, as well. In this play we have both varmints and lions. First of all, Daniel offers to show the power of God to King Nebuchanezzar by destroying the dragon he worships. The stage direction says: "Descúbrese una cueva donde está un dragón grande, echando fuego." Daniel commands the dragon to disappear. No sooner said than done. The dragon drops out of sight, and the cave is screened off from view. Later in the play Daniel is put into a lion's den, a "lago de leones." There probably were many lions there, but we see only two. Abacuc brings food to Daniel, who very generously gives it to the lions. They, we are told, haven't eaten anything for six days. In quite a long scene (here the *gracioso* makes some wise cracks, some of them fairly good) the lions finally bow down ("Humíllanse") before Daniel, who gives them his benediction. The lions go out by one door, and Daniel by another. This play is really quite a treat.

Ruiz de Alarcón does not do much with lions. In *La Cueva de Salamanca*, as one of the tricks of magic, the *gracioso* attempts to embrace the servant. She sinks through the floor, and a lion appears in her place. The lion is embraced instead of the servant. In *La Manganilla de Melilla*, also by Alarcón, Salomon, a Jewish *gracioso* (the only one of that race that the writer has ever heard of) is tied to a tree in a wood. A lion comes along and this time the lion is scared, because Salomon kicks at him, wishing he had "patas de moza gallega."

Vélez de Guevara in *Más pesa el rey que la sangre* has a lion appear briefly on the stage, just in time to help Guzmán conquer a terrible serpent. This lion is eventually drowned in the sea, and when Guzmán describes the sad incident, the author indulges in one of the prize gongoristic passages of all Golden Age Drama. This is the way it goes: Alonso de Guzmán makes his escape from the shores of Africa in a row boat which is a painted "langostín de madera." He reaches a larger boat that is an arrow shot by a bow (the beach) at a target (the setting sun). When the lion finds that he has been left behind, he ferociously shoots himself into the sea (he is first a blunderbuss, and then a marine hippogriff). As the lion hits the water, the level of the ocean rises from the foam and the roars of the lion. The lion next becomes a living boat (*bajel vivo*) and his mane becomes a sail. But alas, the sea is deaf and does not understand the intention of the animal. Instead of a port, the sea gives him a grave.

In one of Calderón's plays, *El mayor encanto amor*, Ulysses lands on Circe's island, and a pack of animals come out to meet him. Among them is a lion, who seems to be making signs to Ulysses to take to the sea again. The intelligence of this lion is later explained, when Circe, at the request of Ulysses, changes the lion back into a man. It was not a real lion, after all. In *Amado y aborrecido* the *gracioso* has a brief encounter with a lion, and makes him leave the stage by calling on Baccus. In *La aurora en Copacavana* Calderón puts some unusual animals on the American continent. When the Spaniards under Pizarro arrive in Tumbez, the Indian chief Yupangí decides to repel the invaders by letting loose the wild beasts that have been assembled for sacrifice. To the surprise of the Spaniards—and to our surprise as well, considering the fact that the scene is laid in South America—a lion and a tiger appear. As these animals approach the Spaniards, they observe that one of the men is holding a cross. At the sight of this holy object the animals tremble and crouch down before the Spaniards. The man who bears the cross caresses them (Los halagan) and the wild animals depart without further ceremony.

A good place to draw the curtain on this display of animal life in Spanish literature is with Calderón's *Los dos amantes del cielo*. In this play the heroine Daría refuses to renounce her Christian religion, and in punishment is put into a house of ill fame. This, of course, is punishment worse than death. As Daría is about to be molested by an impetuous patron of this unholy place, a cry is heard, "Beware the lion." Shortly afterwards a lion enters. He takes his stand in front of Daría, and attacks her admirer. The lion teaches this misguided individual a good lesson, for he bites and scratches him. The roué is really in serious danger, but Daría magnanimously calls the lion off. After this dramatic rescue of shining virtue from darkest sin, the lion leads the girl out of the den of wickedness and guides her out of the city to a cave where she finds her true love, Crisanto. Nice work!

CHAPTER IV

STRIP-TEASE IN GOLDEN AGE DRAMA

As compared with the movies of today the *comedias* of the Golden Age in Spain were lily white, as pure as Ivory Soap, as clean as the driven snow. And yet they were violently attacked by some good souls who didn't believe in letting people have any fun. Among many outbursts it would be hard to find one more vitriolic than that delivered by a certain Fr. José de Jesús in 1601. This worthy friar was a relative of Cardinal Gaspar de Quiroga and rose to be General of the Carmelite Order. He was not "una persona cualquiera." Cotarelo calls him "...uno de nuestros escritores más elegantes y castizos..." Here is a sample of what this man of God thought about *comedias*.

> Es cosa, sin duda, que las comedias, como agora se representan, son cuchillo de la castidad, incentivo de torpezas, seminario de vicios, fuente de disolución, estrago de todos los estados, corrupción de las costumbres, destryción (*sic*) de las virtudes.[1]

Or again, in the same spirit, this worthy divine writes:

> Las comedias que se usan son indecentísimas y grandemente perjudiciales a todo género de gentes porque muy pocas dejan de ser de cosas lascivas y amores deshonestos.[2]

---

[1] Emilio Cotarelo y Mori, *Bibliografía de las controversias sobre la licitud del teatro en España*, (Madrid, 1904), p. 368.
[2] Cotarelo, *Controversias*, p. 370.

Women were on the Spanish stage from the earliest times, but they were supposed to be married and to have their husbands with them. But when it came to actresses dressing up as men, the laws cracked down upon them from time to time in no uncertain terms. For example, we have, among others, the following regulation in 1653:

> ...que ninguna mujer pueda salir al teatro en hábito de hombre, y que si hubiese de ser preciso para la representación que hagan estos papeles, sea con traje tan ajustado y modesto, que de ninguna manera se les descubran las piernas ni los pies, sino que esto esté siempre cubierto con los vestidos que ordinariamente usan, o con alguna sotana, de manera que sólo se diferenzie el traje de la cintura arriba...[3]

Two *alguaciles* were expected to attend each performance and, although their duties seem to have been principally to see that nobody got into the theater without paying and that no men got up in the women's gallery or ventured into the dressing room of the actresses, the responsibility of these minions of the law must have also included seeing to it that actresses dressed as men were modestly attired from the waist down. It must be said that the sight of women dressed as men from the waist up must have been slightly ridiculous, to say the least. How strictly these laws were enforced we do not know, but there can be little doubt that they were evaded more often than not.

But there was one situation which the fussy lawmakers seem to have overlooked. This is where the actress appears "medio desnuda," an early version, apparently, of Gypsy Rose Lee. How many clothes the actresses took off is of course uncertain, but the chances are that they went as far as they dared — and this could have been quite a ways.

Cervantes seems to have been the first to dream up this splendid idea. In *Los baños de Argel* we see Contanza, a Christian captive, who has evidently been dragged out of bed. She is "medio desnuda," but the audience had little opportunity to study her charms, for after only six lines, she departs from the stage and is seen no more in an abbreviated costume.

---

[3] Cotarelo, *Controversias*, p. 635.

Lope de Vega probably had more acquaintance with what we may call "women's natural resources" than any other playwright of his time. He also knew what the public liked, but strangely enough in his plays he shows very little of the stripper. In only two plays out of all those in the *BAE* does he introduce this situation. And even here, he seems to be reluctant to make the most of it. In *La niña de plata* Dorotea is surprised in her bedroom by the Infante Enrique. She appears "en manteo, con una ropa debajo del brazo." Evidently, Dorotea modestly put on a kimona for the occasion.

In *La boba para los otros y discreta para sí* the actress who plays the part of Diana has a chance to appear in three striking costumes: first as a *labradora,* then as a *Duquesa,* and finally in armor (*espaldar y un peto*). In order to put on this armor she has to take off some of her clothes. In having her do so, Lope seems to have been more interested in letting her display some fancy undergarments rather than her own personal charms — "Desnúdase la ropa y basquiña, quedando en jubón rico de faldillas, o almilla bizarra, y naguas o manteo."

Guillén de Castro provides us with three examples. In *Pagar en propia moneda* Elena wants to get unto the jail to free her lover, Prince Pedro de Aragón. To do so, she has to dress as a man. Instead of making the change in the privacy of her room, she does so on the stage, "...se va desnudando, y queda de hombre." In *Donde no está su dueño, está su duelo* Aurelia finds herself in the same predicament as Dorotea in Lope's play. In one version she appears "mal vestida y destocada con una ropa de levantar," and in another, "Medio desnuda." Unlike Dorotea, though, she has no kimona. Castro's *Las maravillas de Babilonia* has many startling details. Here we see a dragon spouting fire, but we need have no fear, for Daniel knocks out this terrifying creature more easily than Cassius Clay did Sonny Liston in Lewiston, Maine. Daniel does not hit the dragon even once, he just talks to him. Clay would have done the same thing to Liston, if the fight had only lasted a little longer. Other spectaculars in this play are Daniel's getting chummy with a couple of lions, and Nebuchadnezzar as a *bestia* eating grass.

This is all quite nice, but there is something even better — There is Susanna "la casta Susana." This charming little lady has a brillant idea. She decides to take a bath. She does not bathe on the stage, probably because there was no shower curtain to hide her, but she does prepare to do so. The stage direction read: "Quítase la más ropa que pueda." The two old codgers from the Bible watch — and no doubt the audience did too, anxious not to lose any interesting detail. [4]

Tirso de Molina seems to have been rather reluctant to associate himself with undressed women. In *La república al revés* we have what becomes a rather common situation where a woman gets out of bed and makes her escape from assassins, "medio desnuda." In *Palabras y plumas* Matilde appears "en ropa de acostar." In *La celosa de sí misma* Doña Magdalena is to be seen "vistiéndose otro traje." In *Desde Toledo a Madrid* Doña Mayor appears "en enaguas," but she is also wearing a *rebociño,* which must have been quite satisfactory to the censors. However, one play by Tirso, *Quien cae no se levanta,* stands in a class quite by itself. Margarita has a different reason for taking off her clothes. She is so moved by a sermon that she rushes out of the church and starts throwing her jewels away, and when these are gone, she starts on her clothes. Her servant Leonela says quite properly:

> Ah, señora de mi vida,
> ¿En la calle te desnudas?
> ¿No adviertes en quien te mira?

Calderón has four plays in which women appear either "medio desnuda" or "medio vestida." Usually they are just getting up out of bed and are not particularly interesting, at least not after what we have seen so far. In *Amar después de la muerte,* though, we have something a little different. Clara is seen "suelto el cabello, sangriento el rostro, y medio vestida." She has been mortally

---
[4] In the little known play *El bruto de Babilonia* Susanna takes her bath off stage, with musical accompaniment (singing). As the elders are about to rush in to do violence to her, she "saldrá a medio vestir." — *El bruto de Babilonia* de Matos, Cancer y Moreto. Librería de Quiroga, 1792.

In the *Susanna* of the *Apocrypha* Susanna sends her two maids for oil and "washing balls," but apparently she does not have time to disrobe before the elders accost her. — R. H. Charles, *The Apocrypha and Pseudepigrapha of the Old Testament in English* (Oxford, 1913), Vol. I, 648.

Parenthetically, Susanna has been a favorite subject with painters.

wounded in battle and manages to talk quite a lot before she finally expires. We are sorry for Clara, rather than interested in her charms.

Rojas is the one who really "goes to town" with semi-naked females. He has almost as many plays of this type as all the other playwrights put together. Some of these plays are of the usual getting-out-of-bed variety, and it must be said that in most cases in the plays of Rojas there is little reason why the ladies are not better dressed, except that Rojas wants them to put on a show. In *Del rey abajo, ninguno* Blanca escapes late at night from the clutches of her husband and appears the next morning "con algo de sus vestidos en los brazos mal puesto" (As a matter of fact, she has had plenty of time to put on all her clothes). In *Entre bobos anda el juego* Isabel comes out into the hall of the inn "medio desnuda" to find her father's room and say she cannot marry Lucas (Why didn't she have a dressing gown?). In *Progne y Filomena* Filomena appears "medio desnuda, con una luz, y una espada en la mano." She has heard someone turning a key in the lock on her door (Why didn't she have the key on her side of the door?) In *El Caín de Cataluña* Constanza sale "a medio vestir." She has had a bad dream (There seems to be no reason why she couldn't have put on a few more clothes, but she looks nice the way she is, and why should we object?). In *La traición busca el castigo* a servant lets Andrés into the house and into Leonor's room. She has heard him in the dark, gets up out of bed, cries out for help, and manages to put on a few clothes. It is interesting to note that the rustle of silk in the dark attracts the attention of the intruder and almost results in her ruin (This situation makes some sense). In *El más impropio verdugo para la más justa venganza* there are two "medio desnudas," one is where Casandra chases Federico out of her room and cries for help. He has raped her. The other is where Diana, "medio vestida," answers a knock on her door and lets a man in, thinking that it is her brother (The lines explain that she has tried to put on something). In *Casarse por vengarse* Blanca makes her appearance "medio desnuda, destrenzados los cabellos, sueltas las basquiñas y una luz en la mano." It is late at night and she has come to ask advice from her father (She could easily have found time to dress a little more elegantly). In *Obligados y ofendidos*, in the very first scene, Fénix is seen "medio desnuda." The Conde de

Belflor has just seduced her and Fénix makes a long speech telling him he should marry her. (She is absolutely right. He should, indeed.) But this is not all. At the beginning of Act Three here is Fénix again, "medio desnuda." She is in the Conde's house this time (It is not at all clear why Clara doesn't have more clothes on. Maybe she liked it that way.)

Rojas introduces a little variation from time to time. In *Lucrecia y Tarquino* "Salen Lucrecia y Julia, dándole de vestir." This is really not very startling, but the point is that it is not necessary to have her appear this way at all. She could just as well have been fully dressed. In *Lo que son mujeres* Serafina is "medio desnuda," for no reason at all except she is at home. In *La hermosura y la desdicha* Juan bribes a servant to let him into Laura's house and Juan gests a genuine, honest-to-God strip tease, for there is Laura "desnudándose, con una luz, que pondrá sobre un bufetillo." She evidently takes off a lot, for she finally says

> Déjame esa luz ahí,
> Porque me quiero acostar.

We have two quite famous characters in *Los áspides de Cleopatra*. In this play Marco Antonio and Cleopatra have been defeated and put in different jails. A friend liberates them, and Cleopatra appears "con un vestido de hombre debajo del brazo." She doesn't need this disguise to make her escape for she overhears an all-important password. When she gets to the shore, though, she "arroja la ropa y una basquiña a la mar," and apparently throws herself into the water, leaving a dagger in the sand. Marco Antonio finds the dagger and writes in the sand "Aquí vive Marco Antonio," and kills himself with the dagger. Cleopatra is not dead, yet. She appears "medio desnuda," having hidden in a cave. She picks some flowers in which, conveniently, there are two asps. She tells them to "feed" on her arm. They do, and when the soldiers find her she makes quite a long speech (26 lines), and "cae muerta sobre Marco Antonio." (Poor Cleopatra, she might have made it to the boat that was waiting to take her and Marco to foreign lands. Perhaps, though, she did not know how to swim.)

Alarcón is missing from our list, and so is Moreto — almost. In spite of almost completely avoiding semi-naked females, he has one scene that is well worth all those that we have mentioned. It is familiar to all students of Spanish literature, but it will bear describing in detail. At the end of Act II of *El desdén con el desdén* Diana, Cintia, Laura, Fenisa, and *damas* are shown "en guardapies y justillos" (Translation: "in their underclothes," or shall we say "foundation garments"). The girls are grouped artistically and the scene is enhanced by songs the girls sing from time to time. The girls are attractive, their abbreviated costumes are colorful and what these costumes reveal is intriguing to a high degree. Here comes Carlos, and how he would like to take a good look! But Polilla is holding a dagger against his cheek and he cannot turn his head. Diana attempts again and again to gain his attention, but to no avail. Finally, she goes to him in person and puts on an exhibit. At this point we are reminded of the almost forgotten advertisement of Lucky Strike cigarettes — "So round, so firm, so fully packed." Carlos has a hard time to make his eyes behave, but he does not peek. The intimate charms of Diana are wasted, not on the desert air, but on Carlos. Here is one striptease that failed utterly, so far as Carlos was concerned, but is not wasted on us.

If there were a contest in taking off women's clothes, Rojas would get credit for the most entries, but Moreto would win first prize for the best exhibit.

Homenaje al Prof. Rodríguez-Moñino, I (Madrid, 1968), 305-310.

CHAPTER V

SCENES OF HORROR IN GOLDEN AGE DRAMA

As compared with the elaborate staging of modern drama, the presentation of plays in the Golden Age of Spain seems rather primitive. There were no wings, no backdrop, little or no scenery, and no front curtain. In one respect, however, the lack of accessories had a certain advantage in that it permitted a change of scene without the necessity of drawing aside, or dropping, a front curtain and moving one set of scenery out of the way to give place to another. The principal emphasis was on the dialogue and the action.

In spite of the almost total absence of visible scenery on the stage, it was possible to attain rather impressive scenic effects. In the back of the stage there was a curtain, sometimes a door, behind which some tableau could be set up, to be revealed at an appropriate moment. The scene behind the curtain could be artistic and beautiful. For example, at the beginning of Guillén de Castro's *Las mocedades del Cid, Primera Parte,* the curtain is drawn aside to reveal "...el altar de Santiago, y en él una fuente de plata, una espada y unas espuelas doradas."[1] Tirso de Molina in *La peña de Francia* makes use of another altar: "Descúbrese una cabaña de ramos en lo alto y en un altar de lo mismo una imagen de Nuestra Señora, con luces...." In his *La Santa Juana, Primera Parte,* the tableau is more striking: "Todas [las mujeres] de rodillas, suena música,

---

[1] Quotations from Calderón, Mejía de la Cerda, Tirso de Molina, Lope de Vega, Ruiz de Alarcón, and Vélez de Guevara are taken from the *Biblioteca de Autores Españoles* and the *Nueva Biblioteca de Autores Españoles*; those from Guillén de Castro from his *Obras* (Madrid, 1925-27).

ábrese una apariencia de la Gloria, Cristo sentado en un trono, el Ángel de rodillas, dándole los rosarios y muchos ángeles alrededor."

Quite as often the drawing of the curtain revealed a scene of horror. A familiar example is to be found in Calderón's *El alcalde de Zalamea*: "Abren una puerta, y aparece dado garrote en una silla el Capitán." [2] Also well known to students of Spanish drama is the ending of Vélez de Guevara's *Reinar después de morir*. Here the author presents a sight that probably was intended to be horrifying, but it could have been just the opposite: "Descubren a Doña Inés muerta, sobre unas almohadas." [3] There is no mistaking the horror in the play by the same author, *Más pesa el rey que la sangre, y blasón de los Guzmanes*: "...descubren un palio negro, y Don Pedro degollado y el puñal hincado junto a él, lleno de sangre...."

Lope de Vega in *El Duque de Viseo* makes use of the curtain: "Descubren al Duque, sangriento, y en una almohada la corona y el cetro, y en otra Doña Elvira, con la mano en una mejilla." Tirso has a startling variation in *Adversa fortuna de Don Álvaro de Luna*: "Descúbrese un teatro de luto, y Moralicos, de luto con un plato pidiendo; el cuerpo [de Don Álvaro] aparte y la cabeza aparte."

One of the most impressive of these disclosures is to be found in Guillén de Castro's *La tragedia por los celos*: "Corren una cortina; aparece Margarita en el hueco de la puerta con una daga hincada en el pecho, y ensangrentada la cara y manos, con dos hachas a los lados." Here we have an added touch in that the torches would light up Margarita's countenance and the flickering light would heighten the horror. Furthermore, the knowledge that this deed was perpetrated by a woman makes the murder all the more frightening. Add to this the fact that Margarita is only partly dressed, and evidently has had no time to give an alarm when attacked by the murderess.

---

[2] Calderón has another *garrote* in *Las tres justicias en una*, "Abre la puerta, que será la de en medio del teatro, y se ve a Don Lope, dado garrote, un papel en la mano, y luces a los dos lados."

Lope de Vega in his *El alcalde de Zalamea*, show two captains dead, though there are no stage directions to this effect. The lines read:

    Alcalde. Descubrid ese balcón.
               Aquí mis yernos veréis.
    Rey. ¡Válgame Dios! ¿Qué habéis hecho?

[3] Cf. Mejía de la Cerda, *Doña Inés de Castro*: "Corren una cortina y parece Doña Inés, difunta, sentada en una silla."

For the sake of the record, a few other examples may be cited: Tirso, *La vida de Herodes,* "Sale Efraím y descúbrese muerto Herodes, con dos niños desnudos y ensangrentados en las manos"; Luis de Belmonte (with others), *Algunas hazañas de las muchas de Don García Hurtado de Mendoza,* "Corre la cortina, y descubren empalado a Caupolicán"; and Guillén de Castro, *Dido y Eneas,* "...descubren la tienda donde está la Reina Dido sobre un trono, atravesada la espada de Eneas por el pecho...." Another striking example is to be found in Rojas' *El catalán Serralonga, y bandos de Barcelona:* "Descúbrese un cadalso con luto, y dos blandones con hachas encendidas, el cuerpo [de Serralonga] sin cabeza, corriendo sangre, y el tronco con capuz, y la cabeza de por sí." Tirso, in *La venganza de Tamar,* presents a very elaborate scene: "Descubren aparadores de plata, caídas las vajillas, y una mesa llena de manjares y descompuesta; los manteles ensangrentados, y Amón sobre la mesa, asentado y caído de espaldas en ella, con una daga en una mano y un cuchillo en la otra, atravesada por la garganta una daga...."

Practically all such scenes of horror are to be found at the end of the plays, but they may occur elsewhere. For example, half way through Guillén de Castro's *Las mocedades del Cid, Segunda Parte,* there is a most unusual situation in which King Sancho is off-stage, defenseless, and Bellido de Olfos hurls a javelin at him with all his might. It is clear that Bellido has not missed his mark, because the King cries out in great pain. After a considerable interval Sancho is brought in, "pasado con el venablo el pecho." Here it must be admitted that under normal circumstances Sancho would have been killed instantly by the terrible weapon. But Castro must not let the King die without allowing him time to confess. To accomplish this, the author gives the dying man 78 lines, spoken on stage, to make amends for his sins before he expires and is carried off by his men, "cubriéndole con la cortina."

In constructing the plays in which such revelations of horror occur, it was of course necessary to allow enough time for the transformation of the living man into an appropriate "corpse." This time element was provided by putting in an intervening scene or scenes. These vary considerably in length. In the first examples of horror quoted, Calderón in *El alcalde de Zalamea* devotes 319 lines to this interval; Vélez de Guevara, *Más pesa el rey,* 100 lines; Lope de Vega, *El Duque de Viseo,* 43 lines; Tirso, *Adversa fortuna de*

Don Álvaro de Luna, 210 lines; Vélez de Guevara, *Reinar después de morir,* 221 lines; and Guillén de Castro, *La tragedia por los celos,* 28 lines. In *Las mocedades del Cid* he has 170 lines in which to allow someone of-stage to perform a rather difficult task, the arrangement of the javelin that pierces King Sancho through and through.

It would seem that 28 lines, or even 43 lines, would hardly be enough to prepare the disclosure of horror that follows. To be sure, the actors could very well slow down their parts at this point of the play in order to give time for suitable adjustments in the case of the "corpse." Here, there is the possibility of making use of a dummy or stand-in. In Lope's *El Duque de Viseo* it seems quite likely that a dummy represented Don Alvaro beheaded. In Castro's *Tragedia por los celos* a stand-in could be so covered with blood that she would not be recognized as someone other than the victim, Margarita.

Once the "corpse" was revealed, the playwrights saw to it that the audience had ample time to appreciate the horror. Calderón in *El alcalde de Zalamea* gives the actors 70 lines during which the Captain in shown garroted; Vélez de Guevara in *Más pesa el rey que la sangre* allows 51 lines to show Pedro with his throat cut; Tirso, *La adversa fortuna de Don Alvaro,* 25 lines, with Don Alvaro on view with his head cut off; Vélez de Guevara in *Reinar después de morir* has 66 lines to present Doña Inés dead on the pillows; and Guillén de Castro, in *Tragedia por los celos,* 34 lines to reveal Margarita all slashed up and gory, if we are to interpret a line in the text, "Antes correré este velo," to mean that the curtain in front of the alcove is drawn back. As an added feature in this case, after Margarita has been shown dead, an eyewitness gives a detailed account (26 lines) describing the shocking deed.

As mentioned above, most of these dreadful sights occur at the end of the play and the final impression left with the audience is one of horror. And the frequency of these scenes makes it clear that they were not objectionable to the audience. On the contrary, the playwrights, one can be sure, were well aware of what the public liked and they did their best to provide it. With very little to work with, they devised effects that could hardly be surpassed in stark realism.

Chapter VI

SOME ASPECTS OF THE GROTESQUE IN THE DRAMA
OF THE SIGLO DE ORO

In the famous romantic manifesto, the *Préface de Cromwell*, Vicotr Hugo gives a large place to the grotesque, which he says plays an immense rôle in the thought of moderns. It is everywhere, he states. On one side there is the deformed and the horrible; on the other, the comic and the buffoon. For Victor Hugo the grotesque was one of the supreme beauties of drama. The French romanticist does not give a clear definition of what he meant by the grotesque, but it is generally understood that he had in mind the juxtaposition of the ugly and the beatiful, the comic and the tragic, for the sake of contrast and artistic effect.

As one example of the grotesque in art, Victor Hugo cites the *gracioso* of the Spanish *comedia*. As we know, this character and his parody of the love affair of his master became practically a dramatic convention in the seventeenth century, to the occasional embarrassment of writers such as Calderón, whose sense of humor was at times somewhat deficient. The *gracioso*, however, was not employed solely for contrast or artistic effect. A large part of his rôle was to amuse the *mosqueteros*, who might otherwise become obstreperous. With Francisco de Rojas and his followers the truly deformed appears to some extent in the *comedia de figurón*, but this type was looked upon not as a form of beauty but as an object of ridicule. Don Lucas de Cigarral, for example, in *Entre bobos anda el juego*, with his long legs, knockknees, bunions, and flat feet, could hardly have evoked anything but laugther. Nor was else than merriment intended.

Certain other forms of the grotesque that can hardly be classified as art appear in the drama of the Siglo de Oro and must have put the managers of that day severely to task to present them satisfactorily. A not infrequent case of this kind is the introduction of lions on the stage, and Lope's *El esclavo de Roma*[1] furnishes a striking example. In this play we see enacted the story of Androcles and the lion. To be sure, the animal does not have so prominent a part as in Bernard Shaw's famous play, but all the same he comes very close to absorbing a major share of the attention after his appearance in the second act. At this point Andronio (Androcles) befriends the lion by removing a piece of an arrow from his paw. The lion is duly grateful and in the next act returns the favor by bringing his benefactor food. We actually see him deliver a rabbit to Andronio. At the end of the play, when Andronio is in the arena awaiting death, the wild beast who is to devour him turns out to be a long-lost friend. Andronio attends to a second and less serious wound, and lion and man embrace for the benefit of the assembled multitude. In commenting upon this extraordinary play, Menéndez y Pelayo says:

> No puede imaginarse argumento más impropio para un drama. El interés recae en el león *filántropo,* cuya presentación en las tablas, que hoy mismo sería difícil empeño para cualquier director de escena, debía de ser problema insoluble en el siglo XVII. Solo la buena voluntad de los espectadores podía suplir lo que a la representación faltaba.[2]

But the problem of presenting lions on the stage was not confined to a single play by any means. Lope's *Adonis y Venus*[3] has two of them. And Guillén de Castro makes a contribution in his dramatization of another well-known story, *Las maravillas de Babilonia.*[4] Daniel is cast into a *"lago de leones,"* and two of its inhabitants come upon the stage. They have not had anything to eat for six days

---

[1] *Obras de Lope de Vega* publicadas por la Real Academia Española... *Obras dramáticas,* VI (1896), 447-84.
[2] *Obras de Lope de Vega,* VI, cxii-cxiii.
[3] *Obras de Lope de Vega,* VI, 3-32.
[4] *Obras de Don Guillén de Castro.* Bibl. de Clásicos Españoles, III (1927), 393-42.

and one might expect they would make short work of Daniel. But no! Food is miraculously brought to Daniel instead, he offers some to the lions, and the wild beasts literally and figuratively eat out of his hand. The *gracioso* makes a few wisecraks and finally:

> Humíllanse los leones, y échales Daniel la bendición, y vanse, él por una puerta, y ellas por otra.

Deserving of fame is the lion that follows Guzmán el Bueno around in Vélez de Guevara's *Más pesa el rey que la sangre*.[5] The presence of this animal is in accordance with the legendary account of the famous Spanish hero, and the author could hardly leave the lion out without destroying a very picturesque element. This particular lion is so friendly that Costanilla, Guzmán's servant, claims that he and the lion eat at the same table and sleep in the same bed. In fact, Costanilla speaks the "lionese" language, so he says, better than Castilian. For most of the play the lion appears to be off stage, but he does appear, if the stage directions are to be trusted, long enough to help Guzmán conquer the terrible serpent. Guzmán's lion is unlucky. When Guzmán finally escapes from Africa the animal is unable to swim as well as Tartarin's camel, and to Guzmán's regret, as well as our own, the boon companion of Costanilla is lost in the water.

Even Ruiz de Alarcón makes an addition to this menagerie. In *La Manganilla de Melilla*,[6] Salomón, one of the few Jewish *graciosos* known to man, is tied to a tree by the Spanish sergeant, Pimienta. While in this predicament, "*Un león llega a Salomón y él se vuelve y tira coces.*" Salomón speaking:

> Muerto soy. A mí se llega.
> ¿No tuviera Salomón
> ¡Cielo! en tan fuerte ocasión
> Patas de moza gallega?

At which the lion departs and is seen no more.

The advisability of introducing a comic character along with the lion was recognized by Calderón in composing *Los dos amantes del*

---

[5] *BAE*, XLV, 95-104.
[6] *BAE*, XX, 303-20.

ciclo.[7] In this play Daría is forced into a *mancebía* because she will not renounce Christ. There she is accosted by Escarpín, whose presence in such a resort is no evidence of virtuous intent. The fair damsel calls upon the Lord to protect her, and at that moment people are heard crying, "Beware of the lion." Strangely enough, the beast enters the house of ill repute, "*pónese delante de Daría y acomete a Escarpín.*" Scratches and bites do not seem to worry Escarpín greatly, but none-the-less Daría eventually calls the wild animal off. The lion then leads her out of the wicked place and guides her to a cave, where she and her lover are reunited in time to be buried alive by soldiers.

If there were any question about lions upon the stage being grotesque, what shall be said about monsters? There are so many of these creatures in the mythological plays of the period that one hardly knows where to begin. Let us take as the first example Lope's *El vellocino de oro.*[8] In this play Theseus and Jason discover the location of the Golden Fleece, which, of course, is guarded by a dragon.

> Aquí se descubre un laurel, y en él el vellocino de oro; á sus pies dos toros echando fuego, y el dragón acometa a Jasón, á quien venza primero, tocando cajas y trompetas.

After concluding this battle, Jason pulls out the dragon's teeth and sows them in the ground.

> Salen cuatro personas armadas de petos y celadas, con muchas plumas, coseletes de un color, y espadas cortas ceñidas, las lanzas plateadas, y dancen el torneo al son de varios instrumentos; y acabado, salgan los toros á Jasón, y él los acomete.

The bulls were indeed considerate to wait so long before making their attack upon Jason and, quite properly, their hesitation is rewarded by death.

Other examples from Lope deserve mention, such as the head of Medusa in *El Perseo*[9] bristling with snakes, and the monster who comes to devour Andromeda in the same play:

---

[7] *BAE*, XII, 235-54.
[8] *Acad.*, VI, 145-71.
[9] *Acad.*, VI, 71-107.

> La sierpe sale echando fuego por la boca, y tocan trompeta, y riñe y queda ella tendida.

In this play Perseus rides upon Pegasus, who might conceivably have been somewhat grotesque in appearance had the stage engineer been at all careless about attaching the wings. It is true that the stage directions do not indicate the necessity of these appendages, but the *Loa* of *El vellocino de oro* clearly states that Pegasus has *"unas alas á los lados."* Like the serpent in *El Perseo*, the famous Python in Lope's *El amor enamorado* [10] was given to spouting flames. They are quite ineffective, however, for Febo attacks the reptile and soon puts him to rout, while the *gracioso* makes excited comment from a safe place. The serpent eventually has his head cut off and Febo brings it in in triumph.

With the advent of Calderón, most of the good stories had already been told, and his only recourse apparently was to tell them again in another way. If we can judge from his *Fortunas de Andrómeda y Perseo*,[11] one feature of his method was to make two dragons grow where one had been before. In this play, for example, the author introduces the seven-haeded Hydra and the three-headed Cerberus. It may be said parenthetically that the appearance of these denizens of the mythological world could not have been very formidable, for they do little except frighten the *gracioso* in a very mild way. Later in the play we see Medusa *"vestida de pieles y la cabeza llena de culebras."* She is chased off the stage by Perseus and then on again, where her head is cut off for our edification. Evidently this performance was effected by some special contrivance, for the head bounces (!) as it strikes the ground. Not satisfied with this exhibition, Calderón closes with another strange and terrible sight. Andromeda is chained to a rock and shortly *"sale un monstruo todo de escamas."* Perseus, content with an ordinary horse without wings (which does not appear, anyway), attacks the strange creature, drives him away wounded, and finally sees him sink in the sea.

The presence of the *gracioso* in so many of the monster scenes makes one seriously question whether they were intended to be taken seriously. But this is not the case with another form of the grotesque,

---

[10] *Acad.*, VI, 71-107.
[11] *BAE*, IX, 631-53.

unadulterated horror, which, as we shall see, is abundant enough in the plays of the seventeenth century in Spain. Let us take Lope's famous play *El castigo sin venganza* [12] as one example. The Duke of Ferrara discovers that during his absence his young wife Casandra has been too intimate with her stepson Federico. Punishment without vengeance, or revenge without the appearance of revenge, forms the basis of a diabolical plan. The offending wife is trussed up and the Duke orders his son to go in and kill "an enemy who has conspired against him." With some hesitation Federico obeys and learns, when it is too late, that he has killed his beloved Casandra. Before Federico can make an outcry, he is set upon by the Duke's servants, who are told that the son has murdered the woman in a fit of jealousy. The servants pursue Federico into the death chamber and kill him. The Duke has been intently watching the whole fearful preceedings from the door, and the audience can well imagine what is going on from the Duke's words and the expression on his face. The situation is intensely dramatic and ought to satisfy all but the morbidly curious. But Lope, evidently foreseeing that someone in the audience might like to see the horrible sight, very conveniently has the Duke want to get a better view, too.

> En tanta
> Desdicha, aun quieren los ojos
> Verle muerto con Casandra.

A curtain in the back of the stage is drawn aside and the two dead bodies are exposed to public gaze. It is not for long, however; only nine more lines are spoken and the play ends.

In Lope's *El rey fingido y amores de Sancha* [13] the curtain is drawn again and we are privileged to see the King of Portugal impaled in proper form. Although this happens to be only a trick to deceive his enemies, the details are intended to make the deception plausible, and blood upon the stake is realistic enough to justify the swoon of the King's promised bride. As a matter of fact, it might well have tried the nerves of some of Lope's audience. In the last act of this play, the wretch who nearly caused the King's death in so horrible a manner is himself caught and punished. A curtain is drawn

---

[12] *BAE*, XXIV, 567-84.
[13] *AcadN*, I, 422-59.

and the guilty party is seen impaled. This time it is not a fake, but the real thing. Although the stage directions do not so indicate, the manager probably saw to it that there was more blood upon the stake this time than there was before.

In *Fuente Ovejuna*,[14] Lope has a whole town rise in revolt against a tyrannical overlord anl lynch him. As evidence that there has been no mistake about it, the head of the offending noble is brought in on a pike and paraded about the stage for our benefit. After this, the authorities make a thoroughly systematic effort to discover the ringleaders. The whole town — men, women, and children — is put to the torture. Here Lope is willing to leave a little to the imagination of the audience. We do not see the actual process of torment, but we can hear the cries of agony from the rack as one person after another is invited to confess.

All these horrors pale before *El prodigioso príncipe transilvano*.[15] In this play, Sigismundo, Prince of Transylvania, is opposed by a veritable host of enemies, both foreign and domestic; but, with the timely aid of Heaven, itself, and a few faithful friends, he triumphs in the end. To say that blood runs freely in this play is a mild statement. In the very first scene two men die a violent death before our eyes, another is put out of business in the next ten minutes, and shortly afterward a curtain is drawn and a tableau is disclosed the like of which would be indeed difficult to discover. Otomán (one of the dead men previously mentioned) is seen half in and half out of a tomb. Around him are grouped other corpses, "as many as the stage will hold," so the stage directions say. We know that there are at least fourteen of them in this bizarre scene because that many have a word or two to say before the curtain falls back and hides them from our view. It would seem as though this sight would be sufficient to satisfy even the most bloodthirsty person, but there is more to come. Numerous attempts are made to assassinate the brave Prince Sigismundo, three more men die on the stage before our eyes, and finally the conspirators are rounded up and sentenced. Here is the stage direction which shows that the sentence has been carried out in quite a satisfactory manner:

---

[14] *BAE*, XLI, 633-50.
[15] *AcadN.*, I, 369-421.

Córrese una cortina y parece el Príncipe en su trono real, en una mano una espada desnuda y en la otra un Cristo, y encima de la cabeza medio arco hecho de catorce cabezas.

One more head (on a pike) is shown after this!

After such a slaughter, the rest of this paper can hardly be else than an anticlimax. But we shall see that, though the blood still flows freely, a few innovations are introduced from time to time. Guillén de Castro, in his *Mocedades del Cid*,[16] takes long chances of making an otherwise impressive scene humorous by having Jimena and Diego Laínez come before the King, she with a handkerchief stained with her father's blood, and he with his cheek wet with gore from the same source. In the second part, *Las hazañas del Cid*, as it is sometimes called, King Sancho is pierced through and through with a javelin, following an extraordinary scene, which eventually was to shock Lord Holland and start a stream of adverse criticism which has continued down to our own day. The wonder is that the javelin in question did not pass clear through the King, for we have seen Bellido Dolfos take a running start in order to make the throw more sure. With such a frightful wound and with the javelin still sticking in him, the King (with help) takes the center of the stage and lives an unexpectedly long time before making his demise.

Guillén de Castro seems to be particularly given to horrible happenings and to be inclined to give a special refinement of his own to them. In *Progne y Filomena*,[17] Filomena has her tongue cut out, and although we do not see the operation (which happens off stage) we do see her torn clothes and her bloody face and mouth. In *Dido y Eneas* the usual curtain is drawn to show Aeneas' sword in Dido's heart, in spite of which she is able to recite sixteen lines of acceptable poetry. In *El renegado arrepentido*,[18] Honorio is disclosed awaiting his turn to be impaled, with two Christians before him who have already suffered that fate. In *El conde de Irlos*,[19] Celinos cuts off Marfira's head before our eyes and throws it down from a wall upon the stage. In *La humildad soberbia*, also by Guillén de Castro,[20] a

---

[16] *Obras*, II, 169-208.
[17] *Obras*, I, 121-64.
[18] *Obras*, I, 206-43.
[19] *Obras*, I, 366-411.
[20] *Obras*, I, 454-501.

table is disclosed with the head of Don Juan upon a plate. After the audience has been sufficiently impressed through twenty-nine lines of verse, we find that the rest of Don Juan is under the table and is properly attached to his head after all. In *El conde Alarcos*,[21] we have a jar of blood for washing the hands at the table, and on the table a plate containing a child's heart. This is pretty bad, but at the end of the play we find that the child has not really been killed. What we saw was only the heart of a lamb.

Tirso de Molina is apparently more inclined to take stories from the Bible as his specialty in horror. In *La venganza de Tamar*,[22] the crime of Amnon against his sister is punished as the Old Testament relates. The usual curtain is drawn aside to let us see the misguided youth at the banquet table with a cup in one hand, a knife in the other, and with his throat cut. The unfortunate Tamar is even advised by Absalom to drink her betrayer's blood! In *La mujer que manda en casa*,[23] Naboth is shown dead with his blood staining the pile of stones on which he is lying. Later Jezebel is thrown down from a tower. Tirso spares us to some extent here, for we do not see her strike the ground, nor do we see the frightful aftermath which the Bible recounts. In *La vida de Hérodes*,[24] Herod is shown dead with two bloody children in his hands. Examples of horror from Tirso's non-religious plays could be cited, but they would be pale beside those already mentioned.

Ruiz de Alarcón stands apart from his contemporaries in many ways, one of which is in this stage business of horror. In only two plays, which after all are literary "stunts," do we find it. Although in *La cueva de Salamanca*[25] he shows a loose human head, it is only a trick, for the head speaks and eventually disappears in a cloud of smoke as one of the marvels of the comedy of magic which this play represents. Alarcón's only real contribution to this chamber of horrors is the surprising scene in *El tejedor de Segovia*,[26] where Fernando organizes a jail delivery at the end of Act I and has to bite off both his thumbs to free his hands from shackles. This feat

---

[21] *Obras*, II, 1-39.
[22] *NBAE*, IV, 407-33.
[23] *NBAE*, IV, 460-88.
[24] *NBAE*, IX, 173-207.
[25] *BAE*, XX, 83-100.
[26] *BAE*, XX, 375-94.

was never duplicated in the *Siglo de Oro,* or at any other time, so far as I am aware.

It is a pleasure to discover that some major playwrights of the century are almost able to refrain from shedding blood. Moreto and Rojas have little or nothing to contribute to this assembly of gruesome exhibits. Vélez de Guevara is not wholly free from this tendency, but his efforts differ from those of all the rest in that the author has in mind an artistic effect. In *Más pesa el rey que la sangre,*[27] after a pathetic scene in which Guzmán refuses to betray the city and save his son Pedro from being killed by the Moors, an outcry is heard from without the gates, and the audience can guess that the Moors have made good their threat. Pedro has been put to death. Shortly after, Pedro is shown, under a black canopy, his throat cut and the bloody dagger sticking in the wound. This may not seem at first sight to be very artistic, but the arrangement of the other characters and the dialogue that follows emphasizes not the horror, but the father's sacrifice and his patriotism as a soldier. Perhaps a better example is *Reinar después de morir.*[28] Doña Inés, slain by two assassins, is shown upon pillows. It is necessary to the plot and the legend to show the dead body, and the ensuing ceremony of obeisance and offering her the crown is an effective dramatic touch, full of dignity and pathos.

We might surmise that this vogue of horror would eventually wear itself out, but such is not the case. Calderón, in whom the drama of the century reaches its climax, is literally steeped in gore. In his *refundición* of Tirso's *Venganza de Tamar,*[29] he not only has Amnon killed at the banquet and shown covered with blood, but he brings in the death of Absalom as well. Absalom is riding through a wood and his hair catches on a tree. This is off stage. Joab finds the unhappy youth in this predicament and thinks he has an excellent chance to put his enemy out of the way. First we see him take a running start and throw a javelin. A cry is heard from off stage. Evidently the missile hit something. Probably Absalom, but he is not dead yet. Joab calls for another javelin and goes off stage to get nearer the living target. Another cry is heard. Joab is obviously

---

[27] *BAE,* XLV, 95-108.
[28] *BAE,* XLV, 109-23.
[29] *BAE,* IX, 401-20.

making a terrible mess of it. Another javelin is requested. No outcry this time. Is Absalom dead? We shall see. The familiar curtain is drawn and poor Absalon is to be seen hanging by his hair with three lances sticking in him.

In *La cisma de Inglaterra*,[30] the body of Ann Boleyn is shown at the foot of the throne she coveted. In justice to Calderón it must be said that the corpse is covered with cloth for a while. In *El mágico prodigioso*, Calderón introduces a real innovation. Two martyrs, a man and a woman, are disclosed in the usual way. This time, through, they are on a scaffold and their heads have been completely severed from their bodies. This ought to be enough, but Calderón evidently did not think so. Lo and behold, above the scaffold is the Devil himself riding on a serpent and making the important announcement to the audience that the souls of the two martyrs have gone to Heaven.

Again and again does Calderón reveal his fondness for bloodshed and tableaux of horror. Quite as impressive as anything we have seen so far is the feat he performs in the famous play *El alcalde de Zalamea*. As every student of Spanish literature knows, the Captain refuses to marry the girl. He knows he is up against a tough proposition in the person of Pedro Crespo, but he relies upon the fact that he is an officer and thinks the uniform will be respected by the civil authorities. He guesses wrong. Pedro Crespo is out to get him, and there are grave doubts whether the marriage proposition was on the square after all. Anyway, Pedro Crespo wins in spite of the threats of that old war horse, Lope de Figueroa, and the flower of the King's army. The curtain is drawn aside, and audience and actors have the pleasure of seeing what a man with a garrote about his neck looks like.

But enough of these fantastic and horrible sights, which could be multiplied if the occasion required. What do they prove? For one thing, they demonstrate that the authors of that day went to strange lengths in their efforts to amuse the audience. It might appear that they were misguided when they tried to introduce lions and dragons, but the popular success of *King Kong* in our own day would tend to prove the contrary. Evidently, almost anything that would give the audience a thrill was considered legitimate, even if there were

---

[30] *BAE*, IX, 215-32.

times when the thrill presupposed, as is the case with the horror scenes, an exceptionally strong stomach. Be that as it may, the audience of the Siglo de Oro clearly had a right to expect from dramatists a great variety of entertainment. And it is very doubtful whether the dramatists, in introducing lions, dragons, and dead men, gave much attention to artistic effect or had any clear idea of what we term grotesque. They were merely giving the public what it liked.

Hispania, XVIII (1935), 77-86.

Chapter VII

NOTES ON THE *GRACIOSO* AS A DRAMATIC CRITIC

The *gracioso* of the *siglo de oro* seldom fails to express himself in a picturesque and original manner, though it must be admitted that sometimes this is his principal recommendation. On other occasions, however, his humor adds color to pronouncements of considerable moment. But when the wit figure enunciates judgments far beyond his experience, we may well suspect that the author is prompting from behind the scenes. Is not this the case when the *gracioso* appears in the rôle of a dramatic critic?

The poor taste of the Madrid audience in matters of drama, for example, is set forth with such feeling by Redondo in Alarcón's *Mudarse por mejorarse* that his remarks seem to reflect an actual experience on the part of the much be-deviled dramatist.

> Comedia vi yo, llamada
> De los sabios extremada,
> Y rendir la vida al quinto;
> Y vi en otra, que a millares
> Los disparates tenía,
> Reñir al quinceno día
> Con Jarava por lugares;
> Y sus parciales, vencidos
> De la fuerza de razón,
> Decir: "Disparates son,
> Pero son entretenidos."
> Representante afamado
> Has visto, por sólo errar
> Una sílaba, quedar
> A silbos mosqueteado;
> Y luego acudir verías

> Esta cuaresma pasada
> Contenta y alborotada
> Al corral cuarenta días
> Toda la corte, y estar
> Muy quedos papando muecas,
> Viendo bailar dos múñecas
> Y oyendo un viejo graznar.[1]

The prominent part which the *gracioso* plays in the *comedias* of the period and the familiarity with which he treats his superiors were common conventions and offered easy targets for criticism. Tirso de Molina, for one, voices his objection to this sort of literary promotion, and even uses the *gracioso* himself to present the protest.

> ¿Qué comedia
> Hay, si las de España sabes,
> En que el gracioso no tenga
> Privanza, contra las leyes,
> Con duques, condes y reyes,
> Ya venga bien, ya no venga?
> ¿Qué secreto no le fían?
> ¿Qué infanta no le da entrada?
> ¿A qué princesa no agrada?[2]

In *Los favores del mundo*, Ruiz de Alarcón seems to be employing the *gracioso* to speak his mind on the same subject.

> Si el cielo no lo remedia
> La sátira encaja aquí:
> Mas no ha de haber cosa en mí
> De lacayo de comedia.
> ¡Cual a la corte pusiera
> Algún poeta, si el caso
> Y el lacayo en este paso
> De la comedia tuviera!
> ¡Cuál pusiera yo a su Alteza!
> ¡Qué libremente le hablara,
> Y qué poco respetara
> Su poder y su grandeza!
> ¡Luego me apartara dellos,

---

[1] *BAE*, XX, 104.

[2] *Amar por señas*, *BAE*, V, 462. Cf. also Gascón in *El prudente celoso*, Ibid., V, 620, and Fuencarral in Castillo Solórzano's *El Marqués del Cigarral*, *BAE*, XLV, 309-25.

> Cuando a graves cosas van
> El y mi amo y Don Juan!
> ¡Mal año! por los cabellos
> De otra parte me trajera,
> Y en todo el caso me hallara,
> Que el Príncipe aun no fiara
> Quizá a los dos, si pudiera.
> Y estando en lo mas famoso,
> Grave, fuerte y apretado,
> Saliera el señor criado
> Con un cuento muy mohoso,
> O una fábula pueril
> De la zorra y el león,
> Y la más alta cuestión
> Concluyera un hombre vil. [3]

With regard to the convenient soliloquy indulged in by master and mistress alike, Rojas has one of his comic figures ironically tell us that its use could be extended even further.

> Yo solamente no tengo
> A quien le cuente mis males;
> Pues vaya de soliloquio,
> Que en cuantas comedias se hacen
> No he visto que las criadas
> Lleguen a soliloquiarse. [4]

Another dramatic device which seems to have evoked considerable comment from the much coached *gracioso* was the happy ending in which marriage arrangements were made for every available couple in the play. Sometimes the servant is so impressed by this practice that he announces the end of the piece even before the first act is finished.

> Y pues con tanta gloria
> Dama y galán se han casado,
> Perdonad, noble Senado,
> Que aquí se acaba la historia. [5]

---

[3] *BAE*, XX, 8.
[4] F. de Rojas, *Donde hay agravios*, *BAE*, LIV, 165.
[5] Calderón, *A secreto agravio, secreta venganza*, *BAE*, VII, 599. Cf. Mengo in Vélez de Guevara's *La luna de la sierra*, *BAE*, XLV, 183; and Copete in Cubillo de Aragón's *El señor de noches buenas*, *BAE*, XLVII, 149.

Or the prospect of marriage convinces him that the second act is the final one.

> Y si el galán y la dama
> Están ya desengañados,
> Aquí acaba la comedia. [6]

As a rule, however, ironical remarks about the wholesale-marriage plan are reserved until the last act.

> ¡Aguarda!
> Ya sabrán vuesas mercedes,
> Que en el punto que se casan
> Las damas de la comedia,
> Es señal de que se acaba. ... [7]

It might seem that this ridicule of practices in which the author himself indulged to a greater or less extent was evidence that the writer in question did not take himself any too seriously. But this hardly seems to be the case. Some examples of dramatic criticism by proxy may be only humoristic touches with no underlying motive; but in other instances, notably with such independent thinkers as Ruiz de Alarcón and Tirso de Molina, the intention is undoubtedly adverse criticism of a technique to which they did not fully subscribe.

Studies in Philology, XXVIII (1931), 315-318.

---

[6] Calderón, *Mañanas de abril y mayo*, BAE, IX, 288.
[7] Calderón, *Saber del mal y del bien*, BAE, VII, 35. Cf. also Beltrán in Pérez de Montalván's *Ser prudente y ser sufrido*, BAE, XLIV, 585.

Chapter VIII

THE *GRACIOSO* TAKES THE AUDIENCE INTO HIS CONFIDENCE

Back along in the early part of this century Raymond Hitchcock, one of America's popular comedians (*King Dodo*, 1902, and *The Beauty Shop*, 1914), had a way of embarassing his fellow actors and delighting the audience by interrupting the play and speaking directly over the footlights. He would say with all seriousness, for example, right in the middle of his part: "You know what I like about this play is that the villains get off so easily." Or, when an automobile horn was heard off stage and a servant announced that the master's car was waiting. Hitchcock might say something like this: "You can't fool me. There isn't any automobile out there. Someone behind the scenes is just blowing a horn."

We have no way of knowing whether the actors of the Golden Age ever interrupted the *comedia* to make some unexpected remark in the Hitchcock manner, but it seems clear that the author sometimes wrote into the play speeches that were intended to have this effect. One can imagine that in such cases the actor advanced to the front of the stage and delivered the prepared speech which was designed by the author to have the appearance of improvisation.

It is impossible to determine who started this practice. Examples appear in plays that appeared at about the same period, and it may have been Guillén de Castro, Alarcón, Tirso, or Lope himself who first endeavored to extract a smile by such an unorthodox procedure. At any rate, an examination of the plays in the BAE, the NBAE, and the Academy edition of Guillén de Castro reveals almost a photo finish with these four dramatists in what appears to be a dead heat.

In *Tragedia por los celos,* if we want to start there, it is not the *gracioso* who indulges in this manner of speaking, but rather old man Galíndez, who listens impatiently to a string of big lies told by the *gracioso,* Godín, and then says:

> Señores, está borracho
> este hombre; por no escuchalle
> no entraré más en palacio.
> *(Obras,* III, 291.)

In *Las canas en el papel y dudoso en la venganza,* supposed by Juliá Martínez to be "una poco cuidada copia de cómicos," it is the *gracioso* who exclaims:

> Señores ¿que diese en mí
> agora este ramillazo,
> *(Obras,* III, 653.)

Alarcón seems to have tried out this device only once, and that in the wild and woolly *Tejedor de Segovia.* The situation occurs in Act II, Scene VI, where the Conde is taking the cowardly *gracioso* Chichón into his confidence. Chichón is quite surprised at this attitude and says first, aside:

> ¿Privado sin merecerlo?

and then:

> Señores, del pie al cabello
> me tengan por alcahuete.
> *(BAE,* XX, 403.)

Tirso also seems to be very sparing of this type of humor. There is one example of only two lines in *Como han de ser los amigos*:

> A qué no obligáis, señores,
> a un leal y fiel lacayo?
> *(NBAE,* IV, 14.)

He introduces something of a variant in *El celoso prudente* (*BAE*, V, 615), where the *gracioso* Gascón addresses the audience as "Caballeros" and recites thirteen lines, plus four lines of a *seguidilla*, which may have been sung if the actor had a voice for it. This is the longest effort of these early authors' indulgence in this practice.

Lope de Vega does not seem very much inclined to have his *graciosos* speak directly to the audience. At least this is the case with the plays in the *BAE*. However, there is one clear example. In *Por la puente, Juana,* Esteban, who, like most of the rest of the men in the play, has fallen in love with the attractive Juana, has this to say:

> Juana me ha muerto, señores,
> Reñí con ella sin armas.
> ¡Qué virotazo me ha dado!
>
> (*BAE*, XXXI, 545.)

A variation of the usual address to the "Senado" at the end of the play is to be found in the closing lines of *Si no vieran las mujeres,* where Tristán begins the last speech of the play as follows:

> Pues, oigan, señoras damas;
>
> (*BAE*, XXXIV, 592.)

Calderón is quite addicted to this form of humor, for we find examples in seven of his plays: *Apolo y Climene* (*BAE*, XIV, 157, 169); *Celos aun del aire matan* (*BAE*, XII, 486); *Dar tiempo al tiempo* (*BAE*, XII, 526); *El escondido y la tapada* (*BAE*, VII, 470); *Fuego de Dios en querer bien* (*BAE*, XII, 332); *Hado y divisa de Leonido y Marfisa* (*BAE*, XIV, 375) and *El postrer duelo de España* (*BAE*, XIV, 145). He has a variety of ways of making these statements to the audience. In *Apolo* he does it twice, once with no one but the *gracioso* on stage and once with two other people present; in *Celos* he has one other person present; in *Dar tiempo,* two other people are present; in *El escondido* it is a female servant, Beatriz, who does the talking, twice in the same scene; in *Fuego* the *gracioso* makes the final speech to the audience, beginning "Señores," in *Hado* it is the *gracioso* with one other person present; in *El postrer duelo* the *gracioso* has a soliloquy of twenty-four lines beginning "Señores." Of these by far the best effort is in *Hado y divisa* when Merlín is brought in by soldiers and left alone with Arminda, who wants him to tell where his master is. In this predicament Merlín seeks the sympathy of the audience:

> ¡Ay, señores, cuál me mira!
> Tengan lástima de mí,
> que soy niño y solo, y nunca en tal me vi.

Rojas limits his use of this device to moments when the *gracioso* gives utterance to some private philosophy. In *Santa Isabel* Tarabilla engages in this exercise and then proceeds to talk to himself for a while (*BAE, LIV,* 268). In *Los áspides de Cleopatra* Caimán has a philosophical speech about how important it is not to get killed and then has a long deliberation with himself about what he is going to do with his life now that he has saved it (*BAE,* LIV, 425). In *También la afrenta es veneno* the *gracioso* indulges in philosophy (*BAE,* LIV, 599) and adds an original touch by addressing the men only ("Señores"), and then the women ("Señoras"). In *La traición busca el castigo* Mogicón recites ninety-four lines of personal philosophy, beginning "Señores," then in the same speech changes to "Reyes míos," and later to "Señores míos" (*BAE,* LIV, 252).

Of the dramatists examined, Moreto is the one who makes the greatest use of this type of humor. *El poder de la amistad* Moclín interrupts a speech to his master on matters of love, to say:

> Señores, ayuda pido,
> porque ésta es causa de todos.
> (*BAE,* XXXIX, 36.)

Two examples (*BAE,* 39:389) ocur in *Yo por vos, y vos por otro,* but they are not notable; and there is one, equally unimportant, in *El defensor de su agravio* (*BAE,* XXXIX, 502). He really "goes to town" in two plays, *Trampa adelante* and *El parecido en la corte.* In the first there are seven occurrences (*BAE,* XXXIX, 146, 149, 157, 162, 163 [two], 165). In *El parecido en la corte* he invents a new use for this device when he employs it to introduce the principal character to the audience:

> Señores,
> este caballero mozo,

> que hoy se apea en esta villa,
> es, por que vean su quimera,
> Don Fernando de Ribera,
> de los guapos de Sevilla.
>
> (*BAE*, XXXIV, 311.)

There are six more examples in this play (*BAE*, XXXIX, 314, 317, 323 [two], 325 [doubtful], 329). In these two plays Moreto establishes a world record, which will probably stand for all time.

P.S.: There is no indication that Raymond Hitchcock knew anything about Spanish drama.

Bulletin of the Comediantes, VII (1955), No. 2, 27-29.

Chapter IX

LOPE DE VEGA AND THE NEW WORLD

If one can judge from the limited number of Golden Age plays that deal with the New World, it would seem that the theater-going public of that period was not particularly interested in the discovery of America and its colonization. Of the plays on this subject that are readily available there are some that deal with the conquest of Chile, and others with the Pizarros and Hernán Cortés.

The plays having to do with Chile are based principally on the *Araucana* of Ercilla and the *Arauco domado* of Pedro de Oña. Almost without exception, these works have at least one scene in with the sound of drums and indiscriminate shooting terrify the Indians. The Holy Cross appears frequently and generally is green, probably to represent the Inquisition. It performs miracles that profoundly impress the Indians. Often a scene depicts the defeat of picturesque demons, or the destruction of horrible pagan idols. Allegorical figures such as Divine Providence, Christian Religion and Idolatry are frequently in evidence. Saint James, mounted on a white horse, is an important ally for the Spaniards in time of trouble. We find a few native words, and these few are synthetic. When they are used in songs, though, they are sometimes fairly effective.

The customs of the Indians are fantastic in the extreme. In *La aurora en Copacabana*, for example, the Indians have such non-American animals as lions and tigers in cages. They are to be sacrificed to the gods. Some of the Indians are well versed in classical mythology, and they refer readily to Apollo, Atlas, Hercules, Phoebus, Venus, Mars and Bacchus.

It is interesting to note that Tirso de Molina in *Amazonas en las Indias* explains why the warlike Indian women can speak Spanish. One of them is an "oráculo, pasmo de esta tierra," who has a gift of tongues. She has taught the Spanish language to her companions and has done so well that her pupils speak better than the women of Seville.

One really terrifying thing about the natives is that they are generally cannibals. Incidentally, human flesh is better when it is roasted. Here is a sample:

> Un cacique, que con rabia
> sacrificando a Valdivia
> asado se lo comió;
> y otros cuatro otra mañana
> sirvieron en un convite
> que hizo a su esposa Aglaura. [1]

In this business of serving up human beings at the table Lope stands at the head with *El nuevo mundo descubierto por Colón*. In one of the scenes the Spaniards make signs to the Indians to indicate that they are hungry. The chief readily understands sign language and straightway gives the following order to his lieutenant Auté:

> Mata, Auté, cuatro criados
> de los más gordos que hallares,
> y entre silvestres manjares
> lo pon en la mesa asados. [2]

As is to be expected, Lope ranks high in the number of works dealing with the New World. He has one *auto* and three comedias that fall into this classification. None of these works show Lope at his best, nor anywhere near it. In fact Lope de Vega fans would prefer not to have these plays mentioned at all. In the case of *El nuevo mundo descubierto por Colón* Menéndez y Pelayo regrets that some foreign critics have considered it representative of Lope: "¿Qué se diría de un crítico español que para dar idea del teatro de Molière reprodujese *la Princesse d'Élide,* o que escogiera por

---

[1] Fernando de Zárate, *La conquista de Mexico,* Sevilla, n. d., p. 9.
[2] Lope de Vega, *Obras,* XI, 367.

modelo del arte de Racine la *Tebaida,* y del arte de Corneille el *Atila* o el *Agesilao?"* [3]

Our consideration of Lope begins with the worst example of all, the *auto sacramental, La Araucana.* This *auto* was not published until Menéndez y Pelayo resurrected it for his edition of Lope's works. It would have been better if he had not disturbed its eternal sleep. He might have done so, had he not been so conscientious. As it is, he calls it: "Una pieza disparadísima, o más bien, absurdo delirio, en que Colocolo aparece como símbolo de San Juan Bautista; Rengo como figura del demonio, y Caupolicán... como personificación alegórica del Divino Redentor del mundo." [4]

The *tragicomedia* of Lope called *Arauco domado* has all the earmarks of a play written to order, or put together in the hope of winning favor from someone who could reward the author in a substantial way. In this case that person was the Marqués de Cañete, son of the leader of the expedition against the Auracanian Indians. It will be recalled that Hurtado de Mendoza was somewhat downgraded by Ercilla and lavishly praised by Pedro de Oña. Lope has all praise for Hurtado de Mendoza. He is an "Alejandro nuevo"

> ...que hurtó la excelsa llama;
> no solamente a Júpiter y a Febo,
> sino a todos los nueve de la fama... [5]

Moratín characterizes the *Arauco domado* in a picturesque way: "...es una de aquellas comedias que escribía Lope después de decir misa, mientras le calentaban el almuerzo. Es sin duda, una de las más desatinadas que compuso: ... indios, indias, chiquillos, soldados, tambores, guitarras, chirimías, cañonazos, asaltos, batallas, *Santiago y a ellos,* y *Cierra España,* y *Viva Carlos, Carlos Viva."* [6]

Moratín may have been unduly severe in his condemnation of the play, although it is indeed far from being among Lope's best. It does abound in grotesque incidents which weaken it no end. Here

---

[3] Lope de Vega, *Obras,* XI, p. cii.
[4] Lope de Vega, *Obras,* III, xvi.
[5] Lope de Vega, *Obras,* XII, 601.
[6] Leandro Fernández de Moratín, *Obras postumas,* III (Madrid, 1867-1868, 135.

are some examples: in order to impress the Indians, Hurtado de Mendoza lies down on the ground so that the priest that carries the Monstrancé can trample on him, or step over him (It is not clear which); Caupolicán and his wife appear in a very refined love scene as they prepare for a bath in a spring; a witch doctor does a fancy conjuring act: "Salga por el escotillón Pillán, demonio, con un medio rostro dorado y un cerco de rayos, como sol, en la cabeza, y el medio cuerpo con un justillo de guadalmecí de oro"; Galvarino is seen with his hands cut off; and Caupolicán's wife upbraids him for being a coward and throws their child down from a height upon the rocks below. All this takes place before the end of the play where Caupolicán is seen impaled. And, believe it or not, he is still able to recite a sonnet and regret that he has been a "bárbaro." He then declares:

> ...estando arrepentido,
> debo creer que en este día he nacido.

And finally, at the very end of the play we have a grandiose tableau. "Salga toda la compañía, muy galana, de soldados, con música, con nueve banderas, y detrás D. García... y sobre una basa se vea, armado con un bastón, el rey Felipe II, muy mozo, como se fuese estatua."

The *comedia El Brasil restituido* is undoubtedly an attempt to cash in on an occasion for national rejoicing. On May 8, 1624, a Dutch expeditionary force appeared off Santos, Brazil, and captured the city. On January 19 of the next year a Spanish fleet left the Canary Islands and on April 28 recaptured the city. It is not clear just when the news of this victory reached Spain, but this rather insignificant feat was celebrated as a great military triumph. By October 23 Lope had finished *El Brasil* and the play was staged on November 6. It is evident that little time was lost by anyone who had anything to do with the play.

It is easy to see that a subject such as the capture and recapture of a city does not lend itself to dramatic treatment. There is too much violent action. Lope attempts to solve this problem by having many of the details of the conflict narrated. But by whom? At first by no less a personage than Brazil itself, who describes the capture of the city by the Dutch. Later on, it is Apollo who tells us about the exploits of the Spaniards and Portuguese. The last scene is rather spectacular; "Arriba se vea un monte con algunas musas y poetas, y Apolo en medio, laureado."

Lope does not let an opportunity like this pass without trying to make friends and influence people. Apollo singles out a host of Spanish and Portuguese heroes and tells about their deeds in considerable detail. And Fame, quite properly, brings the news to "Magno Felipe Cuarto."

A brief love episode, which at first sight seems to be a retake of a famous Spanish legend, turns out to be a dud. Diego de Meneses has seduced a young Jewess, Guiomar, but cannot marry her because of her race. The father of the girl sees vengeance as the only solution and for a while it looks as though the dishonor will motivate calling in the Dutch, just as Count Julian did with the Moors. But no, the Jews in Santos have already done so. All we have is anti-semiticism on the part of Lope.

There are natives in this work, but there is scant justification for their presence. They listen to an account of outrages committed by the Dutch, and we are asked to believe that they would be disturbed by any lack of respect on the part of the Dutch for Christian churches and holy objects. Of course, these Indians prefer Dutch flesh roasted.

A third work of Lope *El Nuevo Mundo descubierto por Colón* has been severely treated by Spanish critics. Moratín considers it a "*comedia* de la más disparatada de Lope," and states that it is a "fracaso, obra de calidad muy inferior." He speaks of "el contraste entre la ejecución, débil, atropellada, superficial muchas veces, y la grandeza abrumadora del asunto."

There is no doubt that the play has many defects, but at the same time it would be difficult to find more elements that would appeal to the uncultured *mosqueteros* of Lope's time. There are many picturesque incidents in the play that could have made it a popular success.

Let us briefly examine some of the scenes that quite likely were received with enthusiasm. It Act I it is impressive to have Columbus tell how he has tried again and again to give up the idea of discovering a new world. Who is he, a poor man "Que vive de piloto." to want to add "otro mundo tan remoto"? Another good scene in this act is where Columbus tells the Portuguese king how another pilot in his dying moments informed him of the existence of a land beyond the seas. The Portuguese king dismisses Columbus discourteously:

> Vete, Colón, y en Castilla,
> (que se creen fácilmente),
> les cuenta esa maravilla.

Later on, there is a splendid scene where El Rey Chico of Granada strolls about the Alhambra with his enchanting Dalifa (nice name) with a background of seductive music. Dalifa no doubt had suitable curves in all the right places, and would well be worth a second look any time.

Another good scene in the act is where the Duque de Medinaceli and the Duque de Sidonia are discourteous to Columbus, calling him "hermano" and "buen hombre," saying that his ideas are Aesop's fables. In still another good scene we see El Rey Chico surrender to Ferdinand and Isabella (cajas y música, here), after which they promise to aid Columbus. This is a splendid way to close the act.

In Act II it is interesting to see the sailors about to rise up and cast Colombus overboard. Fray Buyl intervenes and Colombus says if he does not discover land in three days, they can kill him. The action then passes to America where the reaction of the Indians to the arrival of the Spaniards could well have been of considerable interest to the untutored audience of the time of Lope.

With regard to the last act, Moratín says: "...hay una confusa mezcla de fornicación y doctrina cristiana, teología y lujuria, que no hay más que pedir." It is indeed true that this act is rather risqué in places. The Spaniards make passes at the Indian women, who are not at all reluctant to sell themselves for a handful of shiny beads. This sort of thing evidently gave offense to Moratín, but who can doubt that it was received with enthusiasm by the menfolk in the audience? They would not be easily shocked. And finally, the play ends with a spectacular scene which would be hard to duplicate: "Con música entre acompañamiento, fuentes, y aguamanil, y los indios y los Reyes atrás, y antes de ellos Colón, con una bandera con sus armas y una letra a la redonda."

Allegorical figures in the play such as Imagination, Providence, Religion and Idolatry are not impressive, though they may have been so in the seventeenth century.

The principal and very serious defect in the play is the character of the Spanish soldier Terrazas, a *pícaro* of the worst sort. He is ready to promise anything to the Indian girls, if they will go alone with him into the woods. This is quite what we would expect of him and, deservedly, he comes to a bad end. This is all right, but stangely enough, he is the one selected by Lope to expound to the Indians the advantages of the Christian religion. To have such a rascal preach like this is utterly offensive today, and it is hard to believe that it had any other effect upon the audience of the time.

We have said that the works of Lope that deal with the New World are not his best. And yet they are important examples of his versatility, and they have significance in the history of the Spanish theater. *La Araucana* illustrates how far-away events were sometimes utilized in the composition of the *autos sacramentales*. The *Arauco domado* shows us that Lope was not averse to trying to impress a rich patron (and, let it be a said, he was not alone in this sort of effort). *El Brasil* shows how Lope could seize upon front page news and capitalize on it before it got too cold. And *El Nuevo Mundo* is an example of both good and bad theater, with one thoroughly detestable character. Why Lope had Terrazas preach to the Indians rather than Fray Buyl, who is right at hand, cannot be explained. This *comedia* could have been one of the notable plays of Lope de Vega, rather than an "Almost Was."

Translated from *Mapocho* (Santiago de Chile), I (1963), No 2, 225-30.

Chapter X

A MALIGNED CHARACTER IN LOPE'S
EL MEJOR ALCALDE EL REY

If a poll were taken to select a half dozen plays of Lope de Vega especially notable for their excellence, the chances are that *El mejor alcalde el rey* would be in every list. It was one of the two plays selected as most representative of Lope in the Clásicos Castellanos; it appears in practically every set of Lope's *Obras Escogidas*; and it is always mentioned in any extensive treatment of Lope's dramatic art. Few plays of Lope have had more editions in one form or another. It has been translated three times into French, once into English, once into German, once into Polish, and recently into Italian.

First published in 1635 in the *Veinte y una parte verdadera* of the *Comedias* of Lope, the play was evidently written at the height of the playwright's career. An examination of the play gives evidence of careful workmanship. It has a well organized plot, dramatic situations of great intensity, and characters that are original and convincing. As was usual with plays of the *siglo de oro* this comedia combines tragedy and comedy, and very effectively.

Critics have almost unanimously praised this play for its presentation of the umbridled spirit of the times and for the way Lope has drawn the principal characters. Some critics of the early nineteenth century, however, unduly influenced by their reverence for the French drama of the seventeenth century, note that the play violates the unity of time in a scandalous manner, and occasionally they are shocked at the introduction of humor in so tragic a play.

The character of Feliciana does not seem to have been fully understood by those who have interested themselves in the play. When Dionisio Solís, in one of his many efforts to make the old-time plays of the *Siglo de Oro* conform to new standards and new tastes, rewrote *El mejor alcalde,* he omitted the character of Feliciana altogether, because he though she was "odiosa e inútil."

In 1829 when A. La Beaumelle translated this play into French, he prefaced it by critical comments in which he first speaks of "la faiblesse de Félicie," and then later, says in commenting on Tello: "Sa sœur Félicie ne le blâme que de sa brutalité, et s'emploie à déterminer la jeune fille à consentir à sa déshonneur."

The words of La Beaumelle are repeated by Eugène Baret in his translation of the play (1874), though he limits his comments about Tello's sister to mere mention of "la faiblesse de Feliciana."

It is a German critic, Julius L. Klein, who has the worst opinion of Feliciana. In his *Geschichte des Dramas,* 1874, he speaks of her as Tello's "Leporello in Unterrock." It is hard to see how anyone who had read the play with a reasonable degree of care could go so far as to compare Feliciana to the vile creature Leporello in Mozart's *Don Giovanni,* but Klein evidently could see it no other way.

In 1882 Louis de Viel-Castel in his *Essai sur le théâtre espagnol,* comments as follows on Feliciana: "Félicie qui s'efforce de le calmer en lui donnant l'espérance qu'avec le temps, Elvire pourra devenir moins inflexible." Or again: "en vain Félicie toujours singulièrement accomodante, s'efforce, tantôt de le calmer, tantôt de rendre Elvire moins intraitable."

Menéndez y Pelayo takes a position that is not easily defined. In his introduction to this play, in Volume VIII of the *Obras de Lope,* he mentions the omission of Feliciana by Dionisio Solís and quotes the comment of La Beaumelle, Baret, and Viel-Castel. It would seem that he agreed with these statements, for he says not one word in opposition. Surely, if he had held a different opinion, he would have said so.

Recently, Federico Carlos Sainz de Robles, in his edition of Lope's *Obras Escogidas* (Madrid, 1952), refers as follows to Feliciana, "Dionisio Solís refundió ... *El alcalde,* suprimiendo, por odioso e inútil —en su sentir, que no en el nuestro—, el personaje de Feliciana." But in the same passage he calls her "la abyecta Feliciana," (I, 472), which is certainly no indication of high esteem.

If we turn to the play itself and give attention to its dramatic structure, we can see that the author has set for himself a most difficult problem so far as the element of time is concerned. In the interval between the night that Elvira is abducted and the moment when the king comes to see that justice is done, Sancho must make two trips to court, one to lay the facts before the king and the other to apprise him of the disobedience of Tello. During this time we are asked to believe that Tello has not done violence to Elvira. It is manifestly impossible to provide a strictly airtight explanation for Tello's waiting so long before having his way with Elvira. He has her in his power, his mind is made up, he is all supreme in his own little world, and that is that. The next best thing to a logical reason for Tello's delay in raping Elvira is the semblance of one, and from a dramatic point of view, this is sufficient. This *semblance of an explanation* is Feliciana and her efforts to gain time. In fact, it is the main reason why she is in the play.

There is another weakness in the plot. Before Sancho makes his first trip to see the king, it is necessary from the point of view of logic and common sense that he have absolute proof that Elvira is in Tello's hands. How can we ever think that the king would listen to him otherwise? Here Feliciana comes in handy again. Elvira is in Tello's castle, Sancho is reported at the door, and Elvira is spirited away. When Sancho tells Tello that someone has carried Elvira off, Tello says he regrets that he does not know where she is, that if he did he would see that she were returned to Sancho. At this moment Elvira rushes in:

> Sí, sabe, esposo, que aquí
> me tiene Tello escondida.

What could be more unlikely than for Tello to have Elvira so carelessly confined that she could rush out at this opportune moment? How could she possibly get loose like this and give Sancho the evidence? At first sight, there seems to be no good answer. But at this moment Tello, though there is no stage direction to this effect, evidently turns on his sister, when he says:

> ¿Esto has hecho contra mí?

It seems clear that Feliciana has set Elvira free in the hope of somehow saving her from Tello. Elvira does not gain her freedom, but Sancho gets the evidence he needs.

Except for one speech when Feliciana asks how it is possible to save Elvira from a person so beside himself as Tello, it looks as though Feliciana is siding with her brother in begging him not to treat Elvira so cruelly and in asking him to wait another day before carrying things to extremes. The truth of the matter is that Feliciana knows her brother well enough to realize that she can gain nothing by opposing him directly, that such an attitude will only make him more violent. Her only possible recourse is to pretend to side with him and play for time. Every day gained is a partial victory, and there is always the chance that something will happen to prevent Tello's doing violence to Elvira.

In short, Feliciana is an essential character in the play and her opposition to her brother is a necessary part of the action. Feliciana is never hateful, she never actually helps her brother. She is not weak, or "abyecta." She is anything but the Leporello in Mozart's opera, as Klein would have us believe. Feliciana has been maligned.

Bulletin of the Comediantes, VI (1954), No. 2, 1-3.

Chapter XI

DIVINE JUSTICE IN THE *HAZAÑAS DEL CID*

Critics who have interested themselves in the Second Part of Guillén de Castro's *Mocedades del Cid*, or, as it is more commonly called, the *Hazañas del Cid*, have almost unanimously praised his masterly use of the ballads, his attainment of local color, and the effectiveness of the thrilling combat between Diego Ordóñez and the sons of Arias Gonzalo. Other good qualities less frequently mentioned are the characterization of the Cid, the scenes in Toledo, and the poetical language of the play.

English and American critics, however, have not been overgenerous in their praise of the work, and of these Lord Holland is the most severe. "There are few passages .... which rise above mediocrity. It excites little interest and abounds in improbable and unconnected events.[1] ...." Reading further to discover the reason for Lord Holland's unfavorable attitude, we find that the circumstances attending the assassination of King Sancho struck him as very indelicate and shocked him exceedingly. Nothing in the play, apparently, can atone for such lack of decorum. Ticknor is of the same opinion with regard to the death of Sancho, but he has words of praise for the popular traditions which "break through so constantly" and add a "great charm" to the play.

A few other writers mention the episode of the death of King Sancho, but have only scattered words of commendation for particular incidents. Gassier states that the "apparition shakesperienne

---

[1] *Some Account of the Lives and Writings of Lope Félix de Vega Carpio and Guillén de Castro*, II (London, 1817), 127.

du roi Fernand ... fait une forte belle scène." [2] Menéndez Pidal in his work on the Infantes de Lara speaks of the "emoción extraña" which must have seized all the audience when the voice of Arias Gonzalo was heard warning Sancho against the traitor, Bellido de Olfos. Viel-Castel mentions the miracle of the apparition which saves Zamora, and, in speaking of Bellido, states that he is

> animé de toute l'exaltation d'un patriotisme sombre et sincère, ... il semble que une fatalité plane sur lui, qu'elle l'entraîne a accomplir l'arrêt de la Providence, qu'à cet effet, elle jette dans son âme lâche et perfide quelques étincelles d'un enthousiasme sincère, d'un patriotisme ardent quoique dépravé; c'est bien là la terrible et mystérieuse puissance du fanatisme politique. [3]

Finally, Schaeffer, taking up the idea expressed by Bellido as he hurls the javelin at the defenseless Sancho,

> Cielo, cielo soberano,
> ....
> Esforzad mi corazón,
> pues castigáis con mi mano.

briefly states that Bellido is the tool of avenging justice and fate. [4]

An extended examination of the events preceding the death of King Sancho will show that this episode is worthy of further comment. The first link in the peculiar chain of circumstances which led to the murder of Sancho is found, not in the *Hazañas* but in the *Mocedades del Cid*. It will be recalled that in that play Sancho, following his quarrel with the fencing master, mentions a vague statement by the soothsayers that he will be killed by an "arma arrojadiza" and the cause will be "cosa muy propincua suya." At this point Guillén de Castro makes it clear that even though such a prophecy has been made, it will not necessarily be fulfilled, since astrology is not to be believed, though its predictions should be

---

[2] A. Gassier, *Le théâtre espagnol* (Paris, 1898), p. 81.

[3] L. de Viel-Castel, *Essai sur le théâtre espagnol*, I (París, 1882), 246.

[4] "Wir sehen ferner, wie der Verräther Bellido de Olfos zum Werkzeug der rächenden Schicksalsgerechtigkeit wird, indem er König, Sancho ermordet" (A. Schaeffer, *Geschichte des Spanishchen Nationaldramas*, I [Leipzig, 1890], 220).

feared. In other words, if Sancho is warned and acts aright, the terrible and mysterious blow may be averted.

At the beginning of the *Hazañas,* Sancho's father has died, leaving the kingdom to be divided between the children, Urraca receiving the city of Zamora. Fernando, who has had reason to fear Sancho's rapacity, has given his son warning that a curse will fall upon him if he attempts to disobey his father's will. Sancho, as we know, does this very thing, imprisoning one brother and forcing the other to flee to Toledo. Here it is that the Cid reminds Sancho (and incidentally the audience) of the curse of Fernando. But this warning, even coming from one so important as the Cid, is to no avail, and Sancho proceeds to attack Zamora. At this stage in the action divine justice takes a hand and begins to carry out the prophecy. It must be kept in mind, however, that Guillén de Castro has informed us that the prophecy is not necessarily certain of fulfillment. It seems to be the author's purpose to show that a change of heart on the part of Sancho would have saved him just as surely as did his unchecked ambition bring about his ruin. It is to be noted that Castro again and again repeats that the cause of Zamora is just and that Heaven is on the side of Urraca.

In besieging Zamora Sancho is only too successful, but at the moment when he has victory almost within his grasp Urraca calls upon him to fear the vengeance of his father. To this Sancho replies:

> ¿Tu padre llamas? ¡Para hacerme guerra
> baje del cielo, o salga de la tierra!

In answer to these impious words the ghost of Fernando appears, armed with a bloody javelin, and this apparition, visible only to Sancho, warns him to desist, saying that the weapon before him will be the instrument of his death. Sancho is greatly affected by the strange vision and orders a retreat. At this very moment, though he does not realize it, divine retribution is setting in motion the wheels that will grind him to dust if he does not heed the supernatural admonition. It has chosen for its agent a wretched individual, Bellido de Olfos, and has kindled in his heart a courage and a desire absolutely unknown to him before. With this God-given impulse Bellido hints to Urraca a way to free Zamora and, fired by divine madness, he dares to defy no less a warrior than Arias Gonzalo. The resulting quarrel gives to Bellido's escape to the enemy the appearance of truth.

At the moment when Bellido is in danger of death at the hands of Arias, Sancho is in a state of uncertainty, consulting Diego Ordóñez about continuing the siege. If Sancho is considering abandonment of the attack because disobedience to his father weighs upon his conscience, then a retreat is proper, says Diego Ordóñez, but if it is only through fear of a fantastic vision, then he should go on. Sancho's lust for power is too strong for him and he decides to resume the siege. Here again he openly defies fate by saying if he is threatened with a javelin he will arm himself with one. This defiance finds an immediate answer in the appearance of Bellido who has been miraculously saved from the wrath of Arias:

> el cielo me trajo aquí
> por milagro...

Had Sancho decided differently, Fate no longer needing Bellido, he would have perished at the hands of Arias and his men. The instrument of vengeance and the agent to execute retribution have now been brought together.

As the traitor is about to reveal the weakness of Zamora, a strange occurrence interrupts. The hand of Heaven is giving Sancho another chance to repent as Arias calls down from the walls of Zamora to beware of Bellido. The words of the staunch old warrior have the ring of the utmost sincerity and the king stands bewildered. His words,

> ¿Qué es esto, Bellido?

betray his indecision and the divine courage of Bellido leaves him, since the cause for it (Sancho's intention to disobey his father) is now absent. He is therefore an ordinary mortal, and afraid.

> Ay, cielo,
> De congoja estoy temblando.

And when the Cid supports Arias, Bellido fairly grovels on the ground. But Sancho is not dissuaded by Arias and Rodrigo, both of whom he had every reason to believe, and he decides to listen to Bellido. This act, prompted by the king's desire for power, restores the traitor's courage and he who had trembled a moment before now defies even the Cid. Rodrigo is banished, but warns Sancho that Heaven punishes ungrateful kings.

A few moments later Sancho's momentary decision about trusting himself alone with Bellido again leaves the way open for repentance. But Sancho's desires are too strong for him and the opportunity is lost. (It may be remarked in passing that the extreme improbability of the king's venturing out of the camp alone with Bellido finds an explanation if we admit that Sancho is blinded by desire and led by the hand of fate.) Another possibility of salvation occurs when the Cid, returning from exile at the king's request, passes near the strangely assorted pair. Even this remote chance of change of heart on the part of Sancho dispels Bellido's courage again:

> Tiembla la tierra que piso.

This fear is only momentary, however, for the king turns toward Zamora. Shortly after this, Bellido apparently has his opportunity when he stands behind the king with a dagger drawn, ready to stab him in the back. But Heaven is still giving Sancho time to change his mind. A mysterious something stays Bellido's hand. The king's hour has not yet come and the prophecy has mentioned an "arma arrojadiza" and not a dagger.

Finally, Bellido, owing to circumstances ("cierta necesidad") common to all of us, comes into possession of the javelin and the king is defenseless. Comment on the influence of fate in bringing this about seems unnecessary. Even at this late hour Heaven grants Sancho a moment for repentance since we see Bellido seized with a cold terror which restrains him when he has his arm drawn back to hurl the javelin. Sancho fails to repent and the weapon is driven home, Bellido exclaiming that Heaven punishes by his hand. All that is left now is for the king to acknowledge that his death is just and that neither Bellido nor the city of Zamora is responsible:

> Causa es de causas quien la causa ha sido.
> Fuí hijo inobediente, estuve ciego,
> y el cielo me castiga, ... [5]

---

[5] Just before his death Sancho declares
> La maldición de un padre rigurosa
> en la tierra me alcanza...

And Bellido, having accomplished the will of Heaven, loses his divine frenzy and again becomes a cringing human being to whom is eventually meted out punishment in accordance with the standards of mortals who do not comprehend the hidden and terrible ways of Providence.[6]

If we review the series of steps by which Sancho moved forward toward his doom, we shall see that numerous chances to escape the prophecy are presented to him and, as he disregards these opportunities, the dangers surrounding him increase. After the appearance of his father's ghost, Sancho is in the midst of his men and far from any real peril; at the time of the warning of Arias he is with his soldiers but the instrument of punishment is at hand and likewise the agent of vengeance; after the Cid's warning he is alone with Bellido but still in his own camp; the next time, he is alone with Bellido outside the camp, but soldiers are within hailing distance; finally, the king and Bellido are absolutely alone and all that stands between Sancho and death is the decree of Fate that Sancho shall die by an "arma arrojadiza."

It seems clear that the exaltation of Bellido is not, as Viel-Castel suggests, "un patriotisme sombre et sincère" but the mysterious thrill of an agent divinely chosen for vengeance. This frenzy, dependent as it is upon the attitude of the king, does not always sustain the traitor. Whenever the king even remotely considers withdrawing from the siege, the spirit animating Bellido departs and he finds himself in a very desperate situation. In these moments he becomes his real and cowardly self, appreciating fully the danger he is in and reacting to it in a very natural manner. At other times he is not a free agent and, driven on by something he does not understand, he becomes a superman in courage. As the javelin is driven home, the mission of Bellido is revealed to him, though he does not mention this fact later when he tries to defend his crime to the incensed inhabitants of Zamora.

It may be argued that if divine vengeance is using Bellido as an agent, this mysterious force is guilty of persuading the king to do wrong. Is Bellido, for example, tempting the king when he says he can reveal to him a way to take Zamora? Is this the case, too, when

---

[6] No suggestion of fate or divine justice is to be found in Juan de la Cueva's *Comedia de la muerte del rey don Sancho*.

Bellido again mentions the fact that there is a postern gate which never is closed, and threatens to leave the king and go over to the Moors if Sancho does not believe him? Cases like these, however, either precede or follow some suggestion to the contrary and what is really happening is that Providence, or Divine Justice, is bringing the scales into a fine balance susceptible to the slightest touch. Sancho's most secret thoughts are of vital importance, and upon his decision depends his life.

Hispania, XII (1929), 141-146.

Chapter XII

A NOTE ON THE *BURLADOR DE SEVILLA*

Among the puzzling passages in the *Burlador de Sevilla* there is one which seems at first sight to be an unmistakable error. This occurs in Act II after Don Juan and the Marqués de la Mota have their long discussion of women. Mota moves off and Juan, walking on, hears a signal from a window; a letter is dropped and a woman's voice directs Juan to give it to Mota. Instead of this, Juan opens the note. It is from Doña Ana, the lady the Marqués hopes to marry, and in it she states that her father is planning to marry her to another. If Mota's love is true, he should show it on this occasion. The note continues:

> Por que veas que te estimo,
> ven esta noche a la puerta,
> que estará a las once abierta,
> donde tu esperanza, primo,
> goces, y el fin de tu amor.
> Traerás, mi gloria, por señas
> de Leonorilla y las dueñas,
> una capa de color.

Don Juan resolves to go to the *rendez-vous* in Mota's place and consequently delivers the message verbally in this manner:

> Para vos, marqués, me han dado
> un recaudo harto cortés
> por esa reja, sin ver
> el que me lo daba allí;
> sólo en la voz conocí
> que me lo daba mujer.

> *Dícete al fin que a las doce*
> *vayas secreto a la puerta,*
> *que estará a las once abierta,*
> *donde tu esperanza goce*
> *la posesión de tu amor;*
> *y que llevases por señas*
> *de Leonorilla y las dueñas*
> *una capa de color.*

In his edition of this play E. Barry has the following note to this passage:

> "Une *suelta* dit ici *á las doce abierta,* par une répétition peu naturelle. L'édition de 1630 dit *á las once,* ce qui est une contradiction absolue. Nous adoptons donc le vers du *Tan largo* qui est évidemment le seul bon, car c'est en fixant à minuit pour le marquis un rendez-vous qui est fixé pour onze heures dans le billet de Doña Ana, que Don Juan pourra se substituer à lui." [1]

Américo Castro, in the "Lectura" edition, refuses to make any change beyond putting the line *que estará a las once abierta* in parentheses, adding this comment, "No creo deber corregir este verso, que figura en las ediciones de 1630 y 1649; don Juan debe decirlo aparte y socarronamente; T[an] L[argo], en vez de *a las once* puso *esperando.*" [2]

An explanation of the seeming contradiction in time may perhaps be suggested by the trick of betting on the number of coins on a table. There are actually three. A states that there are four, and B, confident that he can believe his eyes, stoutly claims that there are three. The argument becomes heated and a bet is made. A says, "I insist that there are four coins on the table and you say there are only three. If I am wrong, will you set up the drinks?" B promptly says, "Yes"; and A counters with, "I am wrong. There are only three." In his excitement B did not notice what A was saying and consequently pays for his heedlessness.

---

[1] *El burlador de Sevilla y convidado de piedra.* Paris, 1910, p. 163.
[2] Tirso de Molina. *El vergonzoso en palacio. El burlador de Sevilla.* Segunda edición, muy renovada, por Américo Castro. Madrid, La Lectura, 1922, p. 272.

The situation in the *Burlador* is much the same. Don Juan says,

> Dícete al fin que a las doce
> vayas secreto a la puerta,

and, seeing Mota wrapped in contemplation of the promised state of bliss, carries his boldness to the point of stating aloud in a perfectly normal tone,

> que estará a las once abierta.

In the succeeding lines he may even give special emphasis to *capa de color*, a garment which he hopes to use to supplant Mota. This sort of effrontery on Don Juan's part is like that which he exhibits when he meets Octavio at the beginning of Act II and tells him he was sorry to have left Naples without having said good-bye. Furthermore, it seems to be wholly supported by Mota's next speech, "¿Qué decís?", which indicates that Mota has not been paying attention to a single word that Don Juan uttered after *a las doce*. It is evident that the "Qué decís" is a question since Don Juan replies to it,

> Que este recaudo
> de una ventana me dieron,
> sin ver quien.

Romanic Review, XX (1929), 157-159.

CHAPTER XIII

DID CALDERÓN HAVE A SENSE OF HUMOR?

Dramatic technique of the Golden Age in Spain was more or less standardized by Lope de Vega, whose success with the public was no encouragement for others to deviate from his procedures. And yet, within established broad lines, Lope's numerous rivals developed their own particular talents, some of them very successfully. Guillén de Castro, for example, is notable for his handling of the *romances,* Tirso de Molina for his women characters, and Alarcón for his everyday touches and moral purpose. There are many others who found ways to be original without crossing the loosely set barriers that hedged them in.

One of the elements of the *comedia* most successfully developed by Lope after he had reached the height of his career was the *gracioso.* This character at times has an important part in the action, at other times not. He has something funny to say on most occasions, and his remarks must have contributed no little to Lope's popularity with the crowd. This good lead was followed to some extent by Guillén de Castro, and to a considerable degree by Tirso and Alarcón. In the case of the last two playwrights the *graciosos* are as different from Lope's as two worlds, but they all have one trait in common. They are funny.

Faced with the necessity of amusing a rough and ready audience, the playwright found his *gracioso* a definite asset — provided the character had a sense of humor. But a supposedly funny character that did not live up to expectations could hardly have been anything but a liability to both playwright and actors. At first glance this dreadful handicap seems to have been wished upon Calderón. He appears to have had a comic character thrust into his lap, and apparently he was hard put to make this personage even moderately funny.

If we examine the *graciosos* in the serious plays of Calderón, we find the most ghastly attempts at humor in the whole history of the Spanish stage. In some of these plays, indeed, this particular character could well have been dispensed with, had it not been that Calderón evidently thought that something of this kind was expected. *El príncipe constante* is one of these plays, and here the funniest thing the *gracioso*, Brito, can do is to get trampled on by the Moors, and then in a sudden and unlikely fit of bravery drive the Moors away with a sentence in Portuguese. In *La vida es sueño* the *gracioso* suceeds in getting killed. There is no fun intended in this, the only case perhaps of a *gracioso's* death on the Spanish stage; it merely illustrates one of the philosophical points the author wishes to drive home. But before he passes from the scene this man Clarín springs mediocre joke after mediocre joke based principally upon his own cowardice. The one good bit of humor that he contributes to the gaiety of nations seems to be a wild hit in the dark, the sort or thing that might happen by accident once in a thousand years. When Clarín's "master" Rosaura, in giving up her sword, declares she can surrender it only to a person of high degree, Clarín says to one of the common soldiers:

> La mía es tal, que puede darse
> Al más ruin: tomadla vos.

In the less serious plays, such as those of the *capa y espada* type, Calderón's humor can be quite as uninspired as in his serious efforts. A striking example of an all-out attempt to be funny is to be found in *Casa con dos puertas mala es de guardar*. Here the author has the *gracioso* put on a little play, something in the style of Serafina in Tirso's *Vergonzoso en palacio*. Calabazas thanks his master for giving him a ready-made suit, which will obviate the necessity of having one made by a tailor. The *gracioso* takes two parts, that of the customer and that of the tailor, and for some seventy mortal lines enacts the process of ordering the suit and trying it on. The scene is dull in the extreme, and Calabazas' master evidently thinks so, too, for his comment after it is over is "¡Qué locuras!" Incidentally, it frequently happens that Calderón thus depreciates his own humor.

Examples of this kind could be multiplied, with an assembly of cheap *graciosos*, wooden creatures who are ignorant, unintelligent, and unimaginative. All would be well, and the question could easily be decided in the negative, were it not for a case like *La dama duende*. In this play Calderón presents a *gracioso* who, if not the best in the whole field of *siglo de oro* plays, is without question well toward the front. Cosme, the *gracioso* under discussion, is educated to the point of having seen a number of plays — he is reminded of them by present circumstances; and he is quick witted — when asked to explain why he said he couldn't read (he had made a slip and revealed that he could), he answers that he can read books, but not handwriting. He can curse eloquently — "Doscientos mil demonios De su furia infernal den testimonios..." He carries on a debate with himself about the advisability of going out to pray in a monastery — get a drink in a saloon. He is afraid of ghosts, and there are many humorous scenes in which this trait counts heavily. He has a private philosophy of his own — when his master says the ghost cannot be a demon but must be a woman, Cosme's answer is "Todo es uno." This character has humorous lines, is placed in many humorous situations, and is naturally a funny man in his own right. Cosme is really the best developed character in the play, and there is grave danger of his stealing the show. If one were to judge from *La dama duende* alone, one would say that Calderón was the greatest humorist in Golden Age drama.

Romance Studies Presented to William Morton Dey, University of North Carolina Studies in the Romance Languages and Literatures, No. 12 (1959), 119-121.

Chapter XIV

HUMOR IN THE *AUTOS* OF CALDERÓN

In the *autos sacramentales* before the time of Calderón there is considerable humor of a rough and ready variety. For the most part it is generated by peasants who "horse around," making cheap jokes, usually about being hungry, and griping about their troubles. These humorous characters are pretty much of a piece, with little or no originality, and few, if any, distinctive characteristics.

It is really surprising that Lope de Vega, who reveals a keen sense of humor in his comedias and in them creates genuinely funny characters, should manifest so little of this quality when he wrote *autos*. One of his comic characters in the *autos* is Apetito, "vestido de loco", who makes cracks, for example, in *Las bodas entre el alma y el amor divino* about vegetables and fish. In other *autos* La Gula similarly jokes about food. La Locura, in spite of his name, does not do, or say, very crazy things. Lope's most notable effort in the direction of humor is a *lacayo*, without name, in *Circuncisión y sangría de Cristo*. This *lacayo* is a Roman who for some reason has hopes of becoming Emperor. He does not want to marry a Jewess because it will be bad for his descendants, if they in turn become emperors. This ambitious *lacayo* is greatly shocked at the circumcision of the child Jesus — he thought the ceremony was going to be eating and drinking — and when he learns what it really is about, he is afraid that the officiating parties may start in on him. Really, Lope is more irreverent than humorous in this *auto*.

Tirso de Molina in his *comedias* has a sense of humor of a decidedly vulgar sort and he exhibits some of it in his *autos*. On occasions he has his *villanos* talk a sort of dialect, "Pardiobre" style, and say "mijor "for "mejor" and "huera" for "fuera." They usually complain about the work they have to do. In *No le arriendo la ganancia* the *gracioso rústico*, Recelo, talks about his "bragas rebanadas," and even criticizes the court. In *El Laberinto de Creta* the *gracioso* Risel calls the Minotaur "vino-en-tarros," and says if the Minotaur swallows him, he (Risel) will "escarbar" his "estuémago" and the effect will be that of six pounds of rhubarb. After considerable cheap talk of this sort, Risel gets into the labyrinth and meets the Minotaur, who must have been quite worth seeing on the stage. As is to be expected, Risel has the living daylights scared out of him. In this encounter the Minotaur chases Risel round and round a tree in a scene which must have been funny all right, but it can hardly be said that the humor of the situation is of a very high order.

Calderón has an *auto* entitled *El laberinto del mundo,* but there is no Minotaur in it. In commenting on this *auto* of Calderón and its relationship to Tirso's effort, Valbuena Prat has words of high praise for Tirso's Risel: "El gracioso Risel — que es sencillamente una de las víctimas que habrían de entregarse al monstruo — es quizá el papel más hábilmente tratado, como tal, y el único que merece sobrevivir en el conjunto en la obra. Sus bromas sobre la estructura del laberinto son de lo bueno del Tirso cómico... e igualmente en su temor ante el Minotauro" (Aguilar, p. 1554). [1]

It would seem that only one critic has seen anything humorous in the *autos* of Calderón. Angel Valbuena Prat, in the magnificent Aguilar edition of the *autos* of Calderón, calls attention to the presence of a *gracioso* in a number of Calderón's *autos*. Twenty-seven of the *autos* in this collection have a funny character. Incidentally, there is something mysterious about Calderón's humor, because at times he introduces the most ghastly type of humor in his *comedias,* and at other times he ranks among the best humorists of Spanish drama. [2] In the humor of his *autos* Calderón is never quite as ineffective as he is in some of his comedies, but in two *autos* his performance ranks with his best efforts elsewhere.

---

[1] References to the *autos* are taken from Calderón, *Obras Completas,* III. *Autos Sacramentales.* Recopilación, prólogo y notas por Ángel Valbuena Prat. Madrid, Aguilar, 1952.
[2] See "Did Calderón have a Sense of Humor," *supra,* pp. 101-103.

Calderón has a few run-of-the-mine *graciosos* in his *autos*. There is Zafio in *Las Epigas de Ruth*, who injects a little humor now and then. There is Bato in *Sueños hay que verdades son*, who has a long monologue about being hungry. Bato is something of a language expert, for he argues that if a man who takes care of horses is a "caballerizo," a man who takes care of a "jomento" is a "jomentizo."

Libio in *El Viático Cordero* is a "gitano" who, as Valbuena Prat says, "hace el papel de gracioso no exento aquí de aguda comicidad..." This fellow Libio has a minor part in the *auto*, but he says a few good things. He wants to eat of the Lamb, for example, but Moses forbids him to do so because he is not of the Jewish faith. When Moses tells him he can eat some lettuce, Libio replies: "¿Soy yo / grillo?" (Aguilar, p. 1165).

Valbuena Prat has rather high praise for Almendro in *La humilidad coronada de las plantas*: Almendro... da la nota cómica y realista, de su mero papel de gracioso, que en cierto modo encarna la Locura. De él se hacen

> ...los turrones,
> almendradas para el sueño,
> aceites de almendras dulces,
> almendrones, caramelos
> y peladillas tostadas..."
> (Aguilar, p. 388)

Almendro, however, is not a particularly notable character, though he does rise above the run-of-the mine level once in a while.

There are three *autos* of Calderón in which the *gracioso* has a funny name. One is Morfuz in *Quién hallará mujer fuerte*, dealing with the Bible account of the dirty trick played on Sisara by the "mujer fuerte," Jael. Morfuz has quite a lot to say, largely plays on words that might be funny with a good comic actor in the part, but which are rather flat to read. Unlike the usual *gracioso*, who has little part in the action, Morfuz in this *auto* really delivers the goods on one occasion. This is where he brings in a hammer and nails with which he intends to close up a granary so the food he expects to get will not be stolen. At this point Jael takes from Morfuz the implements with which she plans to operate on poor Sisara. The

Bible does not explain how Jael, who lives in a tent, got possession of these deadly domestic weapons.

Another character with a funny name is Alcuzcuz in *El cubo de la Almudena*; an *auto* in which the Secta de Mahoma, with the aid of Idolatría and Apostasía, fights with Iglesia and is defeated. Alcuzcuz is on the side of the Moors, but he does not relish fighting at all. In the battle he gests a "bota" from a Christian captive, asks another Moor what it is, and the reply is "voneno." Alcuzcuz tries the "poison," likes it, and gets pretty drunk. When one of the Moorish soldiers asks Alcuzcuz why he doesn't get a move on, he replies "If the earth is moving, why should I?" Alcuzcuz' knowledge of Spanish verbs is largely limited to the infinitive forms, and his language is somewhat hard to understand at times, but at the end of the play he surprises us by speaking good Spanish and making a grammatical speech to the audience, asking it to pardon any errors in the play. Alcuzcuz is really quite a pleasant fellow to have around.

Valbuena Prat says that "El papel del gracioso Fará [in *La piel de Gideón*] está desenvuelto con ingenio." This is indeed true. Calderón follows the Bible story fairly closely, but adds some new elements, one of which of course is Fará. Fará is a true *gracioso*, mispronouncing words, reluctant to drink water, and afraid of the enemy. The best thing that Fará does in the way of humor is when he is ordered by Gideon to drink in the river along with the other soldiers. (This in the Bible account is the elimination test suggested by Jehovah to reduce the forces of Gideon and make the Lord's victory really impressive.) Fará drinks standing up so that he can make a quick get-away, if the enemy comes. He is, therefore, completely dumbfounded when he discovers that this act makes him one of the few chosen to get into the fight with the Midianites.

For some reason Calderón has three *graciosos* named Zabulón. One of these, in *El socorro general*, is not very humorous; and another, in *La lepra de Constantino*, is shocking to good taste in his remarks about Christians. However, in *Mística y Real Babilonia*, which deals with the three in the fiery furnace and with Daniel in the lions' den, Zabulón has many good lines. For example, when told that everybody has inherited from Adam "el comer pan con dolor," he answers, "El dolor de no comerle / no heredamos" (Aguilar, p. 1048). When the soldiers of Nebuchadnezzar are about to put a chain on Zabulón's foot, he says they must not do that because he has a "callo" on it. When they try the other foot he says he has a "sabañón" on that, and adds that if he had a third foot, there would be a "juanete" there. An interesting situation in which Zabulón participates is when he is put in charge of the lions. Since he is afraid to open the door of the den, the lions quite naturally get no food, and consequently they are ravenously hungry by the time Daniel is put in with them. When by-standers stupidly wonder if the lions have eaten Daniel, Zabulón says, most appropriately:

> Si ha tanto que más no comen
> los leones que Danieles,
> claro está.
> (Aguilar, p. 1065)

It is usual for many of the characters in the *autos* to have allegorical names, and a frequent character in Calderón's *autos* is Simplicio, Simplicidad, or Inocencia. Sometimes these characters are funny, but as a rule they are not notably so. By far the best is Simplicio in *La primer flor del Carmelo,* in which the Philistines, with Goliath in command, are going to attack the Israelites. When the Philistines ask Simplicio for two lambs, he replies

> ¿Dos solamente?
> ¡Cuatro han de ser, y aun ocho, aun diez y
> aun veinte,
> ciento, trescientos, mil y cuatrocientos,
> centena de millar, cuento de cuentos!

At this point the stage directions call for him to throw everything down and start undressing (Arrójalo todo y vase desnudando, y queda lo más ridículo que pueda.) In keeping with the stage directions, Simplicio continues with his generous offer:

> Y después del ganado,
> el zurrón y la honda y el cayado,
> gorra, sayo, gregüescos y camisa.
> (Aguilar, p. 641)

Fortunately, the Philistines stop Simplicio before he goes too far with his indecent exposure. In spite of this sort of buffoonery, Simplicio is nobody's fool, for at one place in the play he suggests a rather complicated game of naming colors, and he is the one who runs the game.

Another character with an allegorical name is Albedrío, who appears in several *autos*. Sometimes Albedrío is funny, sometimes not. There is an Albedrío in *Psiquis y Cupido,* another in *La vida es sueño,* and another in *El divino Orfeo.* Valbuena Prat has rather a high opinion of the Albedrío who appears in *Andrómeda y Perseo*: "El Albedrío es el gracioso, que al principio de la obra es un loco cuerdo como los bufones de Shakespeare y el personaje cómico de *La cisma de Inglaterra* calderoniana."

A comic character who makes a fairly frequent appearance in the *autos* of Calderón is Pensamiento, who appears in five autos. Pensamiento, dressed in motley colors and in constant movement, jumping around all the time except when the personage whose thought he represents is sleeping, is one of the most interesting of Calderón's comic characters. In four of the five *autos* in which he makes an appearance he does not have much to say or do, but in one, *La cena del Rey Baltazar,* he makes up for the deficiencies of all the rest and really distinguishes himself.

La cena del Rey Baltazar is one of the earliest efforts of Calderón in the field of the *auto*. It is also one of his best. It appears in virtually every collection of *autos,* and has been praised by everyone who has written about it. Valbuena Prat simply calls the Pensamiento in this auto "un modelo de gracioso perfecto." Northup in his school text takes him seriously. He calls him a "clown," who "by word and action shows that human intellect as opposed to faith is an unreliable guide." [3]

As a matter of fact, Pensamiento in *La cena del Rey Baltazar* is much more than a *gracioso* and a "clown." Indeed, in this writer's opinion, the two critics mentioned above have failed to see this character in his true light. Pensamiento is, to be sure, a funny character, and his antics on the stage would certainly be laughable with the proper actor taking the role. But Pensamiento here is much more than just a comic character. In the first place, he is one of the principal personages in the *auto,* representing, as he tells us, Human Thought in general and the thought of Belshazzar in

---

[3] *Three Plays of Calderón.* Edit. with Intro. and Notes by George Tyler Northup. Boston, D. C. Heath, [1926], p. 347.

particular. The principal point to be noted is that he consistently expresses a natural and uninhibited reaction to the situations in which he is placed. He says aloud what any person would think, but under few circumstances would venture to express. For example, when Daniel learns that Belshazzar is going to marry the luscious Idolatría, in spite of the fact that he is already married to the equally attractive Vanidad, Daniel exclaims: "¡Ay de mí!" at which Pensamiento remarks: "¿Habíais de casar con él / que tanto lo sentís vos?" (Aguilar, p. 157). When Idolatría says that she adores 30,000 gods in clay, stone, bronze, silver and gold, Pensamiento is enthusiastic:

> Aquésta sí que es vida:
> haya treinta mil dioses a quien pida
> un hombre, en fin, lo que se le ofreciere,
> porque éste otorgue lo que aquél no diere.
> ... (Aguilar, p. 158)

Later Daniel is threatened by Belshazzar who asks who can protect Daniel against the wrath of the King. Daniel answers this question by saying confidently: "La mano de Dios." Belshazzar is quite taken aback by this boldness but finally pardons Daniel at the intercession of Vanidad and Idolatría. At this, Pensamiento exclaims:

> De buena os habéis librado,
> y yo estimo la lición,
> pues en cualquiera ocasión
> en que me vea apretado,
> sé cómo me he de librar,
> pues sin qué ni para qué,
> "La mano de Dios" diré,
> y a todos haré temblar...
> (Aguilar, p. 164)

Northup objects seriously to these remarks: "This comic speech" he says, "is out of place and spoils a noble scene."[4] This is hardly the case. The noble scene is over before Pensamiento begins to speak, since Belshazzar and his two lady friends have left the stage.

When Belshazzar announces that a georgeous feast has been prepared, and that this banquet will be served in the sacred vessels

---

[4] *Three Plays*, p. 353.

that have been stolen from the temple, Pensamiento says to the King: "Tu gusto alabo." (Aguilar, p. 173).

The best example of the aptness of Pensamiento's thought, and also action, is where Belshazzar and Company sit down at the banquet. Here, Pensamiento, without ado, starts to gulp down the food before anyone else can begin, just as anyone, on seeing good food, tastes it in his imagination before he actually samples it. When Belshazzar starts to drink a toast to Moloch, King of the Assyrians, Pensamiento exclaims:

> La razón haremos;
> sólo hoy me parecen pocos
> treinta mil dioses, y pienso
> hacer la razón a todos.
>
> (Aguilar, p. 174)

In this *auto* Pensamiento is useful in other ways. For one thing, he is the natural intermediary to bring the suggestion of Death to the mind of Belshazzar. For another, when Belshazzar is confused at reading the memorial "Polvo fuiste y polvo eres / Y polvo has de ser..." (Aguilar, p. 168), Pensamiento "anda alrededor de Baltasar," thus dramatizing the state of confusion that the King is in. Finally, toward the end of the play, Belshazzar turns to Idolatría and Vanidad for protection against Death and receives no support. He then addresses Pensamiento, who says, most appropriately: "Tu mayor / contrario es tu pensamiento" (Aguilar, p. 176). In short, Pensamiento in *La cena del Rey Baltasar* is one of the characters that stand out most prominently — and justly so, on account of his apt and humorous remarks.

Without question *El gran teatro del mundo* is far and away the best auto that Calderón wrote.[5] It is, as Valbuena Prat says, "una obra perfectamente construida."

---

[5] Valbuena says that in Spain, since 1927, this *auto* has been given many times. He does not state where or under what circumstances. It was performed at the Summer School of Spanish at Middlebury College in August 1948. According to the *New York Times* it was played in Einsiedeln, Switzerland, during the summer of 1950 from June 24 to September 16. In 1951 in Lima, Peru, it formed a part of the celebration of the Fourth Centenary of the founding of the University of San Marcos; it was played in Barcelona in 1952 during an International Eucharistic Congress; it was put on in English in 1952 by Mount Saint Mary's College in Los Angeles; in Portuguese in 1954 in João Pessoa, Brazil; and in Spanish (a shortened version) in 1955

The Labrador in this *auto* adds immeasurably to the high quality of the play. Nevertheless, this character has been misunderstood by critics.

George Cirot has this to say about him:

"Quant au Labrador, c'est assurément une curieuse figure, inattendue même. Il ne se gêne pas pour tenir de propos inquiétants, voire subversifs:

> No falte en mayo
> el agua al campo en sazón,
> que con buen año y sin rey
> lo pasaremos mejor.

On nous le présente comme un grossier personnage, insensible aux charmes de la Beauté, ainsi qu'il le laisse entendre quand celle-ci retourne:

> No nos falte
> pan, vino, carne y lechón
> por Pascua, que a la Hermosura
> no la echaré menos yo.

Il se sent méprisé; —il sait le sens attaché au mot *villano* par lequel le Monde le désigne:

> Mundo. Tú, Villano ¿qué hiciste" [6]

This critic would, then, have us believe that the Labrador is a subversive individual, almost a Soviet agent, a candidate for McCarthy's committee. He is also, according to Cirot, "grossier," insensible to beauty even when it is right before his eyes.

Alexander A. Parker, in his extensive study *The Allegorical Drama of Calderón*. London, 1943, goes even further in his condemnation of the Labrador:

> "The Peasant is next to perform. His truculence and ungraciousness have already been manifested in the churlish manner in which he received both his *papel* and his *vesti-*

---

by the Dept. of Spanish and Italian of the College of Wooster, Wooster, Ohio. In 1954 William A. Hunter presented a Ph. D. thesis at Tulane with the title "An edition and translation of a Nahuatl version of *El gran teatro del mundo*."

[6] G. Cirot, "El gran teatro del mundo," *Bulletin Hispanique*, XLIII (1941), 295.

dura. He now describes his attitude to his life and work in these terms:

> ¿Quién vió trabajo mayor
> que el mío? Yo rompo el pecho
> a quien el suyo me dió,
> porque el alimento mío
> en esto se me libró.
> Del arado que le cruza
> la cara, ministro soy,
> pagándole el beneficio
> en aquéstos que la doy.

The tone of these lines is one of ingratitude and spite, the earth is kind to him and gives him favors; he turns against her and ill treats her—'Yo rompo el pecho.' It is not that he could do anything else than plow up her face and breast, but he could do it in a different spirit—, he could do it with gratitude and respect." [7]

Parker continues with unfavorable criticism for several pages and concludes: "Calderón does not wish to condone a revengeful spirit in this social class, but he considers it a lesser moral error than the selfishness in the upper classes which produces it."

For Parker, then, the Labrador is truculent, ungracious, ungrateful, revengeful. In short, we may well ask "Who could ever come to like such a creature?" And yet, we find that the other characters in the *auto* do like him, and miss him when he is gone. Why?

Let us examine, in some detail, the part of the Labrador and see if he has the disagreable qualities ascribed to him by Cirot and Parker. The very first thing that the Labrador says, when the Autor announces that he is to play that particular part is "¿Es oficio o beneficio?" (Aguilar, p. 207). Surely, this opening line, with its play on words, was not intended to be serious. The Labrador follows up this remark by asserting that he will be a "mal trabajador," that he suspects he will be a lazy fellow. But since a "No quiero" will be of no avail with an Autor "tan elegante," he will accept the part, but he says he will be "...en la comedia / el peor representante" (Aguilar, p. 208). Since the Autor of the *comedia* is just, the

---

[7] Alexander A. Parker, *The Allegorical Drama of Calderón. An Introduction to the Autos Sacramentales* (London, 1943), pp. 132-133.

Labrador feels sure he will overlook the "poco juicio" of the Labrador. Finally, and most significantly, the Labrador says that he will *play his part slowly, so as not to get tired.* It seems hardly possible that these remarks were intended to be serious. On the contrary, they identify the Labrador from the very first as a chronic, but humorous, grumbler, and they set the tone for an understanding of the part he is to play.

In the representation of the play staged by the characters chosen by the Autor, Calderón gives the Labrador more lines than any other character except El Pobre, who is the figure around which the action turns. Naturally, this personage would have the most lines, since he is so important. The Labrador is, then, the most prominent personage next to El Pobre, and a proper understanding of his character is extremely important.

To continue. When El Mundo is giving out the stage properties, El Mundo asks the Labrador "¿Qué pides tú, grosero?" and the answer is "Lo que le diera yo a él" (Aguilar, p. 210). The Labrador is unwilling to show El Mundo his papel, and this reluctance, with appropriate gestures, would certainly be humorous in the presentation of the *auto*. El Mundo says:

> De su proceder infiero
> que como bruto gañán
> habrás de ganar su pan.

The Labrador's answer is "Esas mis desdichas son" (Aguilar, p. 210). When El Mundo gives the Labrador his hoe, the Labrador says:

> Esta es la herencia de Adán.
> Señor Adán, bien pudiera,
> pues tanto llegó a saber,
> conocer que su mujer
> pecaba de bachillera;
> dejárala que comiera
> y no le ayudara él;
> mas como amante cruel
> dirá que se le rogó,
> y así tan mal como yo
> representó su papel.
>
> (Aguilar, p. 210)

It is extremely hard to believe that this speech is to be taken as a serious utterance.

When the Labrador first appears on the "world stage," he immediately starts griping, as Parker has pointed out, but by this time no one could possibly take him too seriously. Among other things, he complains about the taxes that fall on him, but he says that since he is the one who does the work, he is going to charge for his produce all that the traffic will bear and not stand for any price fixing. He begs God not to let it rain, because in that case he can get even higher prices. At this point Calderón must have thought that he was treading on somewhat dangerous ground, for he softens the remark of the Labrador thus: "pero muy hinchado yo, / entonces, qué podré hacer?" When the Labrador asks this question, La Ley de Gracia prompts him: "Obrar bien, que Dios es Dios" (Aguilar, p. 213). Discreción then asks Labrador if he didn't hear the prompter, and he replies: "Como sordo a tiempo soy," which may be translated into the humorous line: "I am deaf when I don't want to hear." At this point El Mundo comments: "El al fin está en sus treces." The actors, of course, are not supposed to hear what the audience (El Mundo) says, but in this case El Labrador does hear, and he has a definitely humorous reply: "Y aun en mis catorce estoy" (Aguilar, p. 213). The sum total of these remarks would seem to indicate that the Labrador is a comic character, and a very good one, at that.

The Labrador speaks to the audience once again when the King departs. First, El Mundo says:

> ¡Que presto se consolaron
> los vivos de quien murió.
> LABRADOR. Y más cuando el tal difunto
> mucha hacienda les dejó.
>
> (Aguilar, p. 215)

When Labrador is called from the stage, he leaves reluctantly, not because he wants to take anything with him, but because his work is not done. He would like to leave his fields in better shape. He concludes by saying, in anything but a melancholy vein:

> si mi papel no he complido
> conforme a mi obligación,

> pésame que no me pese
> de no tener gran dolor.
>
> (Aguilar, p. 217)

Upon the departure of El Labrador, El Mundo makes what must be taken as an official pronouncement about his character:

> Al principio le juzgué
> grosero, y él me advirtió
> con su fin de mi ignorancia.
> ¡Bien acabó el labrador!
>
> (Aguilar, p. 217)

Not only this, but the characters who are left behind are more sorry to have him go than in the case of the departure of any other character. The Labrador was evidently *simpático*, a pleasant companion, not in spite of, but because of his tart remarks.

The Labrador returns to his complaints when he has to give up his hoe at the end of the "play," but El Mundo is by now accustomed to this sort of talk and makes no reply to his grumbling. Later, the Labrador shows some of his old spirit when the group are all together in front of the Rich Man, who speaks roughly to him. At this Labrador says:

> Deja las locas
> ambiciones, que ya muerto
> del sol que fuiste eres sombra.
>
> (Aguilar, p. 221)

At the very end of the *auto* the Labrador is still in character when he hopes that "bulas de difuntos" will rain upon him and get him out of his trouble.

From the above it seems clear that Calderón intended the Labrador to be not merely a humorous character, but one entirely sympathetic to the audience. As a matter of fact the *mosqueteros* must have been delighted with him. He was one of their own kind, just their style. They would certainly have risen in revolt against any accusation that he was subversive, gross, truculent, ungracious, churlish, or revengeful.

No one has made a careful comparison of Calderón's *autos* with those of his predecessors. When they do, they will probably find that Calderón has a far better acquaintance with the Old Testament than they; that his use of allegory is more profound and more effective; that his characters, though allegorical, are more human, if one can use that word in such a connection; and that his conception of what is dramatic is keener than theirs. It is hoped that this article has demonstrated that in the field of humor and in creating humorous characters, Calderón is so far ahead of the field that the others are merely also-rans, not even in the money for place or show.

Chapter XV

PEDRO CRESPO AND THE CAPTAIN IN CALDERÓN'S *ALCALDE DE ZALAMEA*

The scene in Calderón's *Alcalde de Zalamea* in which Pedro Crespo lays aside his newly acquired staff of justice and tries to get the Captain to marry his daughter has been generally praised by those who have written about it. Typical of the favorable comments is the one by Menéndez y Pelayo in the introduction to Lope's play of the same name:

> A Lope de Vega pertenece, con pleno y perfectísimo derecho, la idea genial de haber juntado en la misma mano el hierro del vengador y la vara de la justicia. Pero Calderón ha ahondado más, y ha sabido encontrar en el alma del terrible Alcalde, juntamente con los furores del pundonor ultrajado y vindicativo, un manantial dulcísimo de afectos nobles y humanos. Antes de proceder como juez, el Alcalde de Zalamea procede como padre: insta, llora, suplica, ofrece de rodillas al capitán D. Álvaro toda su hacienda si consiente en casarse con su hija, reparando el ultraje que la hizo. ¡Cuán lejanos estamos de aquella sutil casuística de la honra, de aquel discreteo metafísico, con que la idea del honor anda envuelta y empañada en casi todos los dramas de Calderón! Aquí, por el contrario, ¡cuán limpia y radiante aparece! ¡Cómo simpatizamos con las lágrimas y con los ruegos de aquel hombre, tanto más sublime, cuanto más plebeyo! No nos encontramos aquí en presencia de un convencionalismo más o menos poético. Son afectos de todos los tiempos, algo que seguirá conmoviendo todas las fibras del corazón, mientras no se pierda el último resto de dignidad humana. La obra maestra de Calderón como poeta dramático, no de una época ni de una raza,

> sino de los que merecen ser universales y eternos, es, sin duda, ese diálogo entre el Alcalde y el Capitán, desde que aquél arrima la vara hasta que vuelve a empuñarla y manda poner en grillos al Capitán y llevarle a las casas del Concejo. Un crítico alemán, Klein, ha llamado a esta escena *el canon de Policleto de la belleza dramática.*
> (*Estudios sobre el teatro de Lope de Vega,* VI, 191.)

It must be said that the non-critical spectator, or the most casual reader, can hardly feel anything but shocked when the staunch old man offers to give the Captain all his property and even sell himself and his son into slavery. This feeling is heightened when the extraordinary offer is climaxed by Pedro's kneeling before the Captain and, with tears in his eyes, begging him to right the wrong he has done.

If we examine the scene carefully, we may well ask: "Does Pedro have any hope that the Captain will accept the offer? Does he think, even for a moment, that there is the slightest chance that the Captain will accede to the request?" If the answer is in the negative, then the action of Pedro Crespo is an empty gesture. Anyone can offer anything, any time, anywhere, if he knows that the other person will not take the proposition into serious consideration.

During the course of the play we have seen that Pedro Crespo is a clear thinker, a good judge of character, and endowed with a vast amount of common sense. He, of all people, should be able to size up the Captain and figure out what his reaction to the proposal would be. The Captain has told him that, even though he is *alcalde,* he has no jurisdiction in the case; Pedro Crespo surely has enough acquaintance with the law to know that the Captain is right; and he must be fully aware that the Captain will not recede from his position. Not only this, but by the time Pedro Crespo actually gets to making his offer, the stony face of the Captain would have made his intentions crystal clear. In short, Pedro Crespo cannot possibly imagine that the Captain will, under any circumstances, marry the girl.

Why, then, does Calderón seem to so demote the proud Pedro Crespo that he practically reverses his character at this point in the play? Incidentally, Calderón does much the same thing with the Captain after Act One, when Álvaro de Ataide, instead of venting his spite on an unruly subordinate, becomes chummy with a man who has got him in wrong with no less a personage than the general himself. There the reason for the inconsistency is to be found in the exigencies of the plot.

There are two answers to the question raised above. The most obvious is that Calderón is giving the actor who plays the part of Pedro Crespo some good lines.[1]

Another explanation is that Calderón, in apparently giving the Captain a chance for his life when Pedro Crespo offers to do everything that is humanly possible, is trying to "condition" his audience to accept without protest the death of the Captain at the hands of an "alcaldillo," as Lope de Figueroa later calls Pedro Crespo. We must remember that the audience is not merely *told* that the Captain is dead. He is seen in a chair, garroted, and there is no doubt about his fate. (When the author of this article has seen *El Alcalde* on the Spanish stage, the horror of this scene was softened and only a shrouded figure was visible, with lighted candles at the head.) The audience of the *siglo de oro* was, to be sure, accustomed to dreadful sights in that back room curtained off from the main stage until the appropriate moment. Nevertheless, in this case an unusual effort must be made by the dramatist in order to have the audience react favorably to a situation in which an officer in the King's army is made the victim of such high-handed justice as that meted out by Pedro Crespo. An added safeguard to a favorable reaction is, of course, the timely arrival of the King, who gives his stamp of approval to Crespo's act.

In the scene between Pedro Crespo and the Captain Calderón was a practical dramatist. He sacrificed a magnificent character in order to be certain that the sympathy of the audience went to the right candidate.

Hispania, XXXVIII (1955,) 430-431.

---

[1] See "Pot-Boilers," *supra*, pp. 24-39.

Chapter XVI

CRACKS IN THE STRUCTURE OF CALDERÓN'S
ALCALDE DE ZALAMEA

Not for a moment would we deny the validity of the many dramatic scenes in Calderón's *El Alcalde de Zalamea*, such as the clashes in each act between Pedro Crespo and Lope de Figueroa, Pedro Crespo's farewell to his son, the arrest of the Captain, and the generous acceptance of defeat by Lope de Figueroa at the end of the play. Nor would we question the splendid characterization of the two excentric old men—except for one instance mentioned later in this study—nor that of the minor characters, Juan, Rebolledo and Chispa.

The construction of Act I of *El Alcalde de Zalamea* is of a very high order. The play begins with a curse that sets the tone of lawlessness that characterizes the play. In the early scenes we see the soldiers griping at their lot, and note their distrust of the officers. Later, the sergeant's effort to keep on good terms with the Captain by billeting him in the house of the prettiest girl in town, his snooping around to find out where the girl is, the Captain's "conspiracy" with a subordinate to see her—all this shows that discipline is anything but well maintained in the army. And yet, back of it all is the stern figure of the general of the army, Lope de Figueroa, clearly a man not to be trifled with, as is seen when he interrupts the conflict in Isabel's room, and is ready to deal out cruel punishment to Rebolledo. In this same scene Pedro Crespo is seen to be a man of strong character, ready to risk his life when his honor is in jeopardy. He, too, is no man to be trifled with. He is, indeed, a worthy counterpart in civilian life to Lope de Figueroa in the military.

Almost all the other characters are no less adequately presented, although some have fewer lines. There is Rebolledo, the troublemaker; there is Chispa, free and easy camp follower; Pedro's son, Juan, something of a ne'er-do-well; and Isabel, the obedient daughter. These characters are clearly drawn. They are interesting. They are individuals, not types.

However, two characters in Act I could well be dispensed with, Don Mendo and Nuño. They add nothing, whatever to the act. In an explanation that accompanies the RCA recording of this play we find this statement: "...se suprimen los personajes del hidalgo Don Mendo y su criado Nuño, por considerar que su intervención, ajena a la línea directa del drama, es menos comprensible si no se pueden ver sus dos figuras, trasunto de las de Don Quijote y su escudero Sancho." With this assertion we are in agreement, except for the reference to Don Quijote and Sancho. The only reason for the appearance of Don Mendo and Nuño in the play in our opinion, is that someone, Calderón or the manager of the company to whom the comedia was sold, felt that there should be a comic part in the play. As a matter of fact, the scenes in which these two characters appear are far from funny, although no doubt they were intended to be. Don Mendo and Nuño hardly appear in Act II, and they fortunately disappear altogether in Act III.

And one more thing is wrong with Act I—no conflict is presented at the end. With Lope de Figueroa's decision to stay in Pedro Crespo's house, everything is settled. That is, everything is settled, unless the Captain persists in his designs upon Isabel. The audience has to wait until the beginning of Act II to learn that the Captain is going to try to see Isabel again, regardless of the orders of Lope de Figueroa.

And here is where the play begins to fall apart. Of course, Rebolledo is necessary to the action later on, but, even so, how can one possibly believe that the Captain would get chummy with Rebolledo after the latter has let him down in the scene with Lope in Act I? Rather, one would expect the Captain to make Rebolledo's life utterly miserable from then on. And this objection is multiplied when Rebolledo says that Lope cannot sleep on account of his game leg and therefore will not be disturbed by a serenade. Furthermore, we are dumfounded when Rebolledo says:

> .... la culpa,
> si se entiende, será nuestra,
> no tuya ....

A second offense on the part of Rebolledo would be fatal, and he knows it full well. Not only this, but would the Captain risk offending Lope by making a disturbance outside the house where he is quartered?

Other minor points. How can one believe Pedro Crespo so indifferent to the election of town officials that Isabel has to remind him of it? And how is it that Juan could wound the Captain and not be cut down by the Captain's henchmen?

In Act III Isabel could tell her sad story in four lines, if not in four words. Instead, she has sixty-seven lines of soliloquy and one hundred and seventy-five more lines in telling her father what has happened. The only explanation possible is that the author has to build up the part of Isabel in order to make it satisfactory to the actress. Up to then she has only a minor part, that of a dutiful daughter, and how can she (the actress), anxious to get her share of the applause, consent to have the two actors who take the roles of Pedro Crespo and Lope de Figueroa get all the good moments? No, that will not do. The author has to give her a considerable number of good lines, and some emotional acting, or else she will not play ball.

The wound that the Captain receives is tricky business. He must be wounded badly enough to be unconscious. Otherwise, he would never have permitted the soldiers to carry him back to Zalamea. He must be well enough to stand up to Pedro Crespo when confronted by him. This last is especially necessary, since the audience must not be permitted to take the side of the Captain and have Pedro Crespo seem to be taking an unfair advantage of a severely wounded man. It is, then, far from clear how serious the Captain's wound really was.

In a previous article ("Pot Boilers," pp. 35-6) we have tried to show that in the scene where Pedro Crespo begs the Captain to marry Isabel the author is "conditioning" his audience to accept without protest the death of an officer in the King's army at the hands of a civilian who has absolutely no jurisdiction in the case —and who knows it.

And while we are on the subject of the execution, is it likely that a peaceful little town like Zalamea would have such a complicated instrument as a garrote to put an end to the career of the Captain?

Hispanic Studies in Honor of Nicholson B. Adams,
University of North Carolina Studies in the Romance Languages and Literatures, No. 59 (1966), 93-96.

Chapter XVII

SOME FIELDS FOR FURTHER RESEARCH
IN GOLDEN AGE DRAMA

Much has been written about the plays of the Golden Age in Spain, but the discussion has dealt mainly with dates of the plays, versification, sources, influences, ideas, philosophy, etc., and relatively little with the actual production of the plays themselves. The writer of this paper has attempted to make a start in this neglected field with the article in *PMLA* (pp. 24-39), in which an effort was made to show that the playwrights were writing to make some much needed money, and that they "dolled up" the plays to make them saleable to the manager of the dramatic company.

But what else is there along the same line that calls for further investigation? Let us begin with the *cofradías* that rented out the theaters. These influential religious orders had a representative at each and every performance to see that no unauthorized person got in free and, more important, to collect the percentage of the "gate" due the *cofradías*. Not all the records of these *cofradías* exist, but do those extant contain, not only notations about the amounts collected, but also the name of the manager of the company, the title of the play, the date of its performance, and even the name of the author?

Before the plays could be performed, they had to be submitted to censorhip. And this regulation raises a good many questions. How were the censors appointed? What were the criteria adopted for permission to present the plays? Are any records of those worthy citizens extant? If so, how much information do they contain?

Even a casual reading of the plays of this period makes us wonder whether the parts were memorized. In the official regulations we find it specified that the censors shall examine the plays "antes que [los representantes] las tomen de memoria." And there is frequent mention in one place and another, in Rojas' *El viaje entretenido* and in Pérez Pastor's *Nuevos datos,* for example, to rehearsals. Rojas seems to indicate that before the rehearsals the actors spent considerable time studying:

> Pero estos representantes,
> Antes que Dios amanece,
> Escribiendo y estudiando
> Desde las cinco a las nueve,
> Y de las nueve a las doce
> Se están ensayando siempre.

Can it be that these lines mean that at the ungodly hour of five in the morning the actors were copying off their parts and memorizing them? No other mention of such goings-on has appeared in the research performed for this paper. On the other hand, the contracts with the players state again and again that the actors shall attend all the rehearsals at nine o'clock in the morning and that they will be fined if they do not show up. Evidently, this sort of preparation for the presentation of the plays was serious business.

All this tends to show that the plays were memorized. But if we examine the plays and note the long speeches in many of them, it seems inconceivable that these parts could be learned except by persons with an exceptional memory. And among the innumerable actors on the Spanish stage, many of them with little education, it hardly seems that there could have been a wealth of memory wizards.

And this is not all. The companies had very extensive repertories. There is record, for example, of Antonio de Rueda, not one of the most popular *autores de comedias,* agreeing in 1639 to give ninety *representaciones* in Sevilla, in the course of which there were to be each week "dos comedias jamás vistas ni representadas." Is it likely that the actors could memorize all these plays and have them ready in the time specified?

There are references to prompters (*apuntadores*), who did not get as much salary as the actors, and whose duties included making posters advertising the plays. But just what were their duties otherwise? Can it be that they read off the whole play to the actors, as is frequently done on the Spanish stage today, and the actors picked up the lines on the fly and repeated them back to the audience?

It must be confessed that it would be very difficult to find satisfactory answers to questions such as these, but even so, it might be well to assemble all the evidence and see what it adds up to.

Managers of companies, such as Nicolás de los Ríos, Gaspar de Porres, Baltasar Olmedo, and Cristóbal de Avendaño, were very active and seem to have been extremely popular. There is available a good deal of information about these men, such as contracts with the actors, with the city fathers, and notations in the plays themselves. More needs to be written about these men and their relations with the playwrights of the time.

Of these managers perhaps the most interesting is Nicolás de los Ríos, "the first of the *graciosos*," says Lope de Vega. Evidently, he was a good actor as well as manager. A study of the relations between him and Lope and Cervantes would be a valuable contribution to our knowledge of the period. Incidentally, a very interesting article could be written about his being banished with his company from Madrid for a whole year because he presented a play which give offense to the French ambassador. What was the play, what was objectionable in it, and who was the touchy ambassador?

A study of dramatists that are lesser known than Lope, Tirso, Alarcón and Calderón would throw light on the period under consideration. And with regard to the dramatists about whom so much has been written, there are still some details yet to be discovered. For example, how was it that Alarcón failed to get his degree from the University of Mexico? And who wrote the first part of Alarcón's *Tejedor de Segovia*? This first part, presumably not by Alarcón, was supposedly written after the second part. A detailed study of the first part of this play in a recent article by J. A. van Praag does not seem to settle the question. One of the reasons for the hostility of the other dramatists to Alarcón may have been his acquaintance with people of high degree. Is there anything in the letters of these aristocrats that bears upon the life and work of Alarcón?

Tirso de Molina is credited with having written some 400 plays, and yet we have only about 80. If he actually wrote 400, this is a higher percentage of loss than is the case with any other playwright. Is there any explanation for this loss?

There was a spurious Part Five of the plays of Calderón, of which two editions appeared in 1677, one in Barcelona and one in Madrid. Does this Part Five deserve further study? And what about the relationship of Calderón and Vera Tassis, who claimed to be "su mejor amigo," when he published an edition of Calderón after his death?

A number of years ago J. B. Trend did a lot of work on music in the plays of the Golden Age. What has happened to his notes? Are they available, and if so, what do they contain?

Another possible field of investigation might be the interpolated stories (anecdotes) scattered through the *comedias* of the Golden Age.

If these remarks should happen to inspire anyone to investigate one or more of these topics, the spirit of this writer would rejoice exceedingly.

South Atlantic Bulletin, March, 1969.

The Department of Romance Studies Digital Arts and Collaboration Lab at the University of North Carolina at Chapel Hill is proud to support the digitization of the North Carolina Studies in the Romance Languages and Literatures series.

www.ingramcontent.com/pod-product-compliance
Lightning Source LLC
Chambersburg PA
CBHW020420230426
43663CB00007BA/1247